To Teri,

My Soul mate

My Light,
My Love,
My Life, &
My source of ShaLom

Light, Love, Life, Shalom

Published by:

Blooming Twig Books LLC

PO Box 4668 #66675

New York, NY 10163-4668

www.bloomingtwig.com

ISBN 978-1-933918-57-0

First Edition

10 9 8 7 6 5 4 3 2

Acknowledgments-Gratitude

This book has been a 20 year project. It has evolved along with me over those years. Some people have had a heavy impact on that evolution. Some people have had just a minor impact. I have neither the space nor the memory to properly thank each of you for gifting a part of you to me. I hope that each of you gets a chance to read this book and that I can give back to you some of what you gave to me. As I point out in the book, gratitude is one of the keys to happiness. I am going to aspire to a lot of happiness by having gratitude and expressing thanks to a lot of people. Please honor these people by reading these acknowledgments.

I want to thank my family. My wife, Teri, to whom this book is dedicated, has given me 34 years of loving support in our marriage. Although I am sure that she often thought to herself, "just shut up and do it," she has patiently encouraged me at every step along the way. My children, Debbie, Zahava, Zev, and Bassie have been willing subjects as I have tested my ideas on them over the years. They are always in the front of my cheerleading section, and I love them dearly. My daughters are blessed with three wonderful husbands (that's one husband each!). In chronological order, Zahava married Daniel Berman, Debbie married Michael Feder, and Bassie married Joshua Zysman. The support and love that these men give to my daughters is amazing to behold. They have also been sounding boards for my ideas, giving me excellent feedback.

Next I want to thank my mother and father, June and Arnold Steinberg. These are two of the most incredible people I know. My mother is my happiness hero, my model of how to be happy and achieve happiness.

She has taught me the joy of life. My father is my dental professional mentor. He has modeled for me how to be a lifetime learner in search of professional growth. This book would not be possible without their encouragement and assistance. I am lucky to have a wonderful mother-in-law, Zelda Chapnick. She has always been interested in hearing the parts of my book as they have evolved. I have always had the backing of my sisters, Barbara Robinson and Ruth Gleicher, as well as my brother, Mark Steinberg. They and their spouses, Jay Robinson, Amit Klein, and Julie Steinberg have listened to my ideas and given me tremendous feedback, and I appreciate that deeply. A special thank you goes to Jay who spent many hours helping to edit the book.

It is hard for a writer to survive the experience without close friends. These are people who stay with you through thick and thin, through the good and the bad. I want to acknowledge Marsha and Dr. Andrew Rosenson, Dr. Sherri and Dr. Jeffrey Bressman, Aviva and Dr. Philip Greenland, and Miriam (Of Blessed Memory) and Rabbi Jerold Isenberg. Miriam, who just recently passed away, was one of my biggest fans. She was privy to some of my earliest writing. She made helpful comments and offered encouragement along the way. For most of her adult life, Miriam suffered from serious medical conditions. She modeled courage, strength, dignity, kindness, and deep trust in God, regardless of her condition. Those of us who knew her were truly blessed.

I have had many excellent teachers in my life. In particular I want to express my appreciation to Dr. Judith Heilizer, Dr. Charles Greene, Dr. Gerald Schroeder, Rabbi Milton Kanter (Of Blessed Memory), Rabbi Saul Berman, Rabbi Yehiel Poupko, Rabbi Mark Gottlieb, Rabbi Barry

Robinson, and Rabbi Gerald Teller. Rabbi Teller and I have been Saturday morning study partners for more years than I have been writing this book. There were plenty of times when we discussed the book more than the text at hand. It's been my privilege to be both his student and his friend over the years.

Five people in particular have given me professional support and guidance over the years. I want to thank Lloyd Shefsky, Amy Morgan, Jody Catalanello, Milton Salzer , and Daniel Uditsky for the mentoring, teaching, and professional assistance. Their stories lead to my story.

I am grateful to my speaking coach, Juanell Teague, and her team. Juanell took me through the surprisingly challenging path to becoming a keynote speaker. She taught me how to make many of my esoteric ideas take concrete form. She is a model of living life as a loving servant of others, with its source in deep faith. Her associate, James Huggins, taught me many tricks of the trade that have been of help.

I want to thank all the people at the National Speakers Association, both on the national level and at the local Illinois chapter. Special thanks go to my colleagues in Seasons of Speaking, our local mastermind group. In particular, a huge thanks to Deanne DeMarco who spent part of her vacation reading the final draft and advising me on how I could make the book better by making one more draft!

While we're at it, I want to thank several individuals, unmentioned as of yet, who read and made significant comments on parts of the manuscript at different points in its evolution. Dr. Sheila Bender read my first chapter years ago, and many of her comments remain solidly in place. Jeffrey McHugh not only assisted with some early editing, but did some research as well. Sally Shields helped with one of the later editions.

This project would never have come to fruition had I not met Kent Gustavson the publisher of Blooming Twig Books. I met Kent at a National Speakers Association convention. We spoke for hours. He told me he believed that my idea could become a great book. He never wavered in his support. He was cheerleader, coach, editor, advisor, and all-around good sport. His assistant, Amber Bean, was available 24/7 for any help needed for the book. His Editor, David RuizdelVizo, was of tremendous help. David put in extra time and effort so that I could have an index. His layout person, Tamas Kato, made my words appear as nice on the page as they did in my mind. I will never be able to thank Kent and his team enough for having made my dream come true.

Dreams do come true, but not as quickly as we wish, and never without pain and problems. I am grateful to the Power & Loving Greater Than Ourselves, to God, for the blessing and challenge of writing this book. Blessed are you God king of the universe who has given us life, sustained us, and brought us to this time.

TABLE OF CONTENTS

— INTRODUCTION —

I am a dentist with Parkinson's disease. How's that for an oxymoron? A dentist with Parkinson's disease! That's right up there with an *exact estimate* or *governmental efficiency*. The only oxymoron I know that beats it is *jumbo shrimp*!

Sadly, it was because of Parkinson's disease that I had to retire from the clinical practice of dentistry. I loved dentistry. I could take someone who was in pain and make that pain end. I could treat someone who could not chew, and after I was finished with their treatment they could go to a restaurant and enjoy a meal. I could take someone who would not smile because her teeth embarrassed her and create a smile that restored her self-esteem. What's more human than a smile? I was able to create smiles all day long, and I loved it. Every day I would wake up with purpose and look forward to another day filled with meaning, joy, and inner peace. But then I had to stop.

That led me to ask the question, **"Why me?"**

"Why me?" My friends tell me I'm a nice guy. I've done my fair share of volunteer work and community service. I am also an observant Jew. I observe the Jewish Sabbath, and I keep kosher. So I ask again, with even more emphasis, **"Why me?"**

I've got another question, **"Why you?"**

At some point you have experienced some significant setback, along with every other human being. Each of us has encountered difficulties in our lives. Each of us has suffered pain. Each of us has faced problems, tests, obstacles, challenges, and unmet goals or expectations in our lives, both at work and at home. Each of us has made painful mistakes. Each of us, at some point, has wanted to cry out the obvious question, **"Why me?"**

When you ask, **"Why me?"** you're essentially asking, "Why is life so difficult? Why do I suffer from pain and problems? What is the meaning of that suffering and the purpose of those problems?" Life is filled with challenges that must be overcome to achieve happiness.

So then, **how can we achieve happiness— joy and inner peace— in the presence of these challenges?** This book is an attempt to answer that question. This book can be your roadmap along *Your Path to Happiness*

Not only am I a dentist with Parkinson's disease, but as a speaker I am also known as "The Values Doctor." As "The Values Doctor," I can help you overcome challenges and achieve happiness by using the healing power of timeless values. Life is a terminal condition. There is no cure. We will all die. We can, however, heal. By focusing on the four key healing values of Light, Love, Life, & ShaLom, I will show you how to discover your unique purpose at work and at home. Using a set of "Prescriptions", the tools from the system that I call *Your Path to Happiness*, I will show you how to discover the unique value you add to the world. I identify that as your primary healing value. Thinking and acting on purpose and using your primary healing value as a guide will allow you to overcome challenges and achieve happiness, joy, and inner peace (or shalom).

To experience joy and inner peace— to achieve that SHALOM — you must:

Solve problems
Heal pain
Address needs
Look to satisfy wants
Overcome challenges
Make opportunities

AT WORK
&
AT HOME

As a result of using the Path Prescriptions from *Your Path to Happiness* at work, you will learn how to shift your team's focus, as well as your own, from complaining about problems to creating and implementing extraordinary solutions. You will create value for your customers while addressing their needs and satisfying their wants. You will combine *spirituality* and *science* to overcome challenges and create opportunities. You will transform your business from ordinary to extraordinary.

You will attain more money and meaning from your work. At home you will learn how to create an environment of love, respect, responsibility, communication, teamwork, fun, and growth. Both at work and at home, you will be empowered to heal from life's pain, accomplish more goals, achieve more success, and, most importantly, reach greater happiness.

I realize that this is quite a claim to make. How will *Your Path to Happiness* accomplish all of these things? The key to the system, **The Primary Path Prescription**, is: **using timeless values for thinking and acting on purpose.** Thinking and acting on purpose lead to happiness. ***Happiness is the joyful actualization of your meaning and purpose.**** Happiness cannot be pursued directly or achieved instantaneously. It must ensue from searching, finding, and acting on purpose. When you uncover your purpose— the meaning and values of life which are of unique importance to you—you also uncover your reason to be happy. *The power of purpose overrides the pain of problems,* thus empowering you to be happy in any moment.

What can be confusing is that happy and happiness are two different words. We mistakenly take them to represent the same idea. **Happy is what you choose to <u>be</u>; happiness is what you choose to <u>become</u>.**

We are not only human beings; we are also human becomings. Our mission is to be happy while becoming someone who realizes happiness.

The realization of happiness is a process of achieving your purpose over time. While you pursue this achievement, you have a reason to be happy because you are doing what you are meant to do. You are helping others through your unique talents and abilities. You are using your primary healing value, and that, in turn, heals you as well. You're doing what you enjoy doing and doing it well. You are serving other people.

Once you have a reason to be happy, which is your powerful inner source of value, meaning, and purpose, you can be happy at every moment. Finding and living by this reason requires taking a special path through life searching for truth—thinking on purpose— and doing the right thing— acting on purpose. This book contains that path. Understand, though, that as long as we are alive we never finally arrive in a permanent state of happiness. Once we overcome one challenge, another one rears its ugly head. Then, once again, we must think and act on purpose; we must remain on our path to happiness.

Which is more important— thinking or acting? The answer is "Yes!" Both are equally important. If we do not understand, we cannot act properly. However, no matter how well we think, thinking alone is insufficient for success. We must still eventually act. This is a world of practical reality where results matter.

This conflict between thinking and acting leads to a paradox. A paradox is two seemingly conflicting or contradictory statements that, on a deeper level, simultaneously seem to be true. For example, are we good, or are we evil? Again, because of paradox, the answer is "yes." Paradox exists in story, not in philosophy. In philosophy, we need to resolve paradoxes; you can't have contradictions. In life, paradox remains a reality; paradox is a part of our story. Therefore, this book will include story and philosophy. Story is simply a better way of understanding life itself. Philosophy works best in metaphysical thought, in the realm of timelessness. We will discuss that realm and address philosophical issues. However, here in life, in this world where there is change through time, story works better. In this book, I will relate to you my thinking and my acting. I will disclose my philosophy and my story in my quest to answer the question, **"Why me?"**

"Why me?" is a three-part question:

1. Why do I suffer from pain and problems?
2. Why do I exist? What is my purpose? What value do I add to the universe?
3. Why am I in business? What is the purpose and meaning of my work?

Answering those questions and acting on the answers lead to overcoming challenges and experiencing happiness. Through telling you my story and philosophy, I hope to empower you to improve your story and your journey through life.

Throughout this book we will focus on the primary path prescription: using timeless values for thinking and acting on purpose. The first half of the book will focus on thinking on purpose; the second half of the book will focus on acting on purpose. Through both thinking and acting on purpose, we will try to understand and answer the three-part question, **"Why me?"**

We have these and similar questions deep inside of us. Left unanswered, left unaddressed, they can lead to pain and problems, feelings of brokenness, imbalance, unhappiness, depression, and lack of inner peace. These questions come to us from a part of us that is beyond our bodies and even beyond our minds. They come not from the physical but from the metaphysical (literally beyond the physical). These questions come from our souls. To connect with these deep questions is to connect with that which is beyond our purely physical selves and beyond nature. We can connect with the power and love within us that can make judgments, access values, know right from wrong, and create freely-willed choices. We can connect with that part of us which is holy. Connecting to that power and love literally permits us to live lives of meaning and value, to become holy. It is the source of discovering our purpose or our mission. Without it we remain broken and unable to heal.

We live in a society and in a time of heavy emphasis on secular materialism. It is a powerful philosophy based on science alone. Science is a wonderful tool, and we will see just how important it is. However, it is not the only tool and should not be used alone. It can lead you to believe there are only matter and space, atoms and the void. Nothing exists that's outside of human sense perception or experimental instrumentation. You think that you have non-physical emotions, but science will say, "Sorry, but that is just the dance of the molecules in your brain." Yet hidden, but perceived and unseen yet sensed at some level, there is a second world, another dimension. That dimension is of a Power & Loving Greater Than Ourselves. Many of us refer to that as God. I do. There are many other names and terms that people use for the concept that I call God; names such as: the oversoul, the super-conscience, the creator, Brahma, Krishna, Shiva, Adonai, Elokim, Hashem, Theos, Christ, Allah, Shangdi, Ahura Mazda, Jehovah. All of these are just different ways of acknowledging a Power & Loving Greater Than Ourselves or a higher dimension. Each unique name represents a unique idea or path for thinking and acting in relation to that Power & Loving. Gandhi believed that as there are many paths leading to the top of a mountain, so there are many ways to God. Rabbi Jonathan Sacks pointed out, "One of the most profound religious truths Judaism ever articulated was that God loves diversity; he does not ask us all to serve him in the same way."[1] He continues, "That is why, though there is one God, there are different ways of finding Him."[2] Each brings a distinctive set of solutions to what are considered the key questions of life.

In this book, often, but not always, I will present a traditional Jewish viewpoint. That is my path up my mountain, my path to happiness. Use it as you see fit. Using my Jewish viewpoint, I use the name of God. Feel free to use any name that you find appropriate.

This second world of a Power & Loving Greater Than Ourselves may be more "real" than our material world of space and time. Our world may be, as Plato proposed, shadows of the light of a more ideal world.[3] It is a metaphysical dimension: a world of spirit, a world of ideas, a world of consciousness, and a world of the four key healing values: Light, Love, Life, & ShaLom.

In short, it is a holy world. This dimension contains spiritual Light and is the source of truth, of right and wrong, of eternal ethical and moral standards, and of timeless values by which we can judge our actions as well as those of others. This Light embodies *thinking on purpose*. Our job as human beings is to connect with that second world, to that Power & Loving Greater Than Ourselves. We are to bring the spiritual Light and timeless values of that world into our productive lives and into this material world. We are then to transform our world, not transcend it. We transform this material world through acts of service and love.

The first half of the book is entitled *Thinking on Purpose* and contains 5 chapters.

In Chapter 1, I tell you my story, **"Why Me?"** Then we begin to investigate your story, **"Why You?"** Through these stories we uncover a preliminary answer to the question, **"Why Me?"** In Chapter 2, we introduce a powerful tool for thinking on purpose: *The Lessons of Learning.* Emergent from those lessons are three timeless values: freedom, responsibility, and purpose. These principles will form a basis for understanding how to learn.

Chapter 3 focuses on the *Universal Whole-Parts Whole Process.* Understanding this process gives us deep insight into the source of our pain and problems in our life. Out of this source also come solutions in the form of *Your Path to Happiness* and the four healing values of Light, Love, Life, & ShaLom.

Chapter 4 clarifies our thinking about happiness. Do you need success to be happy? Do you need to have a life free of problems to be happy? Is it better to have positive or negative expectations towards happiness? What is the difference between being happy and achieving happiness?

Chapter 5 completes the section of thinking on purpose. It poses the question, **"how do you know?"** When searching for truth and looking for understanding, how do you know when you have found it? You must take my course, "Knowing 101," which will teach you how to climb "The Ladder of Learning."

The second half of the book is entitled *Acting on Purpose*, and it contains four chapters detailing *Your Path to Happiness*. One chapter is devoted to each of the four healing values: Light, Love, Life, & ShaLom.

Chapter 6 is entitled *Search for Light; Finding Your Purpose at Work and at Home.* Here we discuss making the Timeless Values Connection; that is, connecting to the spiritual Light from the Power & Loving Greater Than Ourselves and using that light to discover your unique purpose here on earth.

Chapter 7 is entitled *Act with Love; the Sacred Path of Serving Others.* Through acts of love and service and through the use of the Golden rule, we connect with each other and with the Power & Loving Greater Than Ourselves. We are not talking about Love, the feeling; we are talking about Love, the value. Customer service and serving our families are both based on the tool of listening with love.

Chapter 8 introduces *Moments of Encounter.* Life is a journey through moments of encounter along *Your Path to Happiness.* These moments are opportunities to engage the spiritual potential in our physical space-time universe. Responsibility is the ability to accept what is and choose a response that is extraordinary in any moment of encounter. We choose our path to happiness in those moments. The significance of expressing gratitude as a fundamental value and principle for a life of happiness as we pass through any moment of encounter is emphasized.

Chapter 9 is entitled *Seek Happiness & ShaLom; Staying on the Mat at Work and at Home*. This final chapter summarizes the book by focusing on how to achieve happiness, or shalom. ShaLom is usually interpreted as peace. It can be used as hello and goodbye (peace be with you when you come, peace be with you as you go). Peace can be seen as simply a time without war. However, it signifies far more. The Hebrew word shalom comes from the root shalem, to be made whole. To have ShaLom is to have balanced, harmonious unity. ShaLom is joy and inner peace. It is happiness. It is valuing each unique part and its contribution to the harmonious whole. If everyone played first violin in a symphony orchestra, would it work? Of course not. We must value differences, not simply tolerate them. I help you with my strengths, talents, and abilities while you help me with yours. We must take the parts, the **challenges** of our universe, and unite them. We must take this broken universe and reconnect the parts once again into a balanced harmonious whole. By combining Light, thinking on purpose, with Love, acting on purpose, we get a Life of thinking **&** acting on purpose with moments of ShaLom— moments of healing, joy, inner peace, and happiness. This book contains *Your Path to Happiness*— your path to maximizing moments of joy and inner peace— using the healing power of the four values: Light, Love, Life, & ShaLom.

Search for **Light**.
Act with **Love**.
Create a Holy **Life** &
Seek **ShaLom** - Happiness

Part One

Thinking On Purpose

— CHAPTER 1: —
"WHY ME?" MY STORY

SUNDAY MORNING JUNE 24, 2001. It was a beautiful morning for a bicycle ride, one of the highlights of my week. Although you cannot tell by looking at me now, I was once a triathlete and tournament level racquetball player. I have always valued physical activity, but I no longer had time to compete. Each Sunday morning, however, I was reliving the competition in my mind's eye, while enjoying the beauty of the ride.

That morning I had no idea what was ahead. I had a discussion with my wife about some plans for the next month. Little did I realize that those plans would never come to pass. I went outside, put on my helmet, waved goodbye to my neighbor, and off I went. The first half-hour of that particular Sunday was uneventful. The first mile or two I rode in a very easy gear, spinning away happily. Soon I was pedaling up Sheridan Road, a historic lakeside street north of Chicago.

With the wind in my face, my legs pumping rhythmically, and my whole body leaning into the ride, I quickly hit my stride. I felt that familiar feeling wash over me that I was borderless and free. As a dentist, I spent my days working in confined spaces, making small precise movements. Trekking on my two-wheeler provided a release where I could expand and feel a part of something larger.

I did notice more traffic than usual, so I took care to stay curbside. When I rode on a street like Sheridan Road, I took care to look down for potholes and then up for cars and bikes. Down and up, down and up. As I was looking down then up, down then up, I took a quick peek at Lake Michigan. Already it was dotted with boats sailing peacefully in the morning sun. Down and up, down and up. I hardly noticed a van passing on my left as I approached Elder Park. Down and up, down and up. The air was fresh, the grass was green, the trees were magnificent, and summer flowers were bursting with reds, yellows, and pinks. Down and up, down and... Suddenly I noticed that the van had turned right in front of me!!!!!! I had one second before impact. The Power & Loving Greater Than Ourselves, God, took my hands and helped me to turn the handle bars to the right, presumably to avoid the inevitable crash.

Now, I thought about this later. This is God we are talking about. He could have done any of a number of things to make the crash less inevitable. God could have made the van disappear. At least he could've made the van a lot softer, like a marshmallow. Perhaps he could've supplied my bike with airbags. He could've done anything; he is God, for God's sake. One of the lessons in life that we will discuss later is having gratitude. In reality, the move did save me from being impaled by those handlebars. For that I am eternally grateful. I squeezed hard on the brakes, but it was too late. At 18 mph I smashed into the van.

I experienced the impact as if in a dream, watching myself. I felt my shoulders touch and remember thinking to myself, "Self, that can't be good." My helmet slammed into the side of the van, my body bounced off, and I miraculously landed on a very small patch of grass. I knew then that God had decided my time here was not finished. Oh, by the way, I did make a rather impressive dent in the side of the van.

Out of the van jumped the young driver who was, of all things, a lifeguard. I asked him to take out my cell phone from my pack and call 911 and then my wife. He mentioned to my wife on the phone that he thought I would stop. Right, stop with 1 second of notice. Later it turned out that he had had his license for a mere six days. My luck.

At the hospital, several sets of x-rays were taken. A doctor came in and said, "Your x-rays are quite remarkable!" You do not want to hear the word remarkable applied to your x-rays. I want my x-rays to be boring, dull, or average, anything but remarkable. I was diagnosed with two broken collarbones, five broken ribs, and a broken scapula, the big bone at the top of the back. The doctor said he had not seen a broken scapula all year. Remember, it was already June. Glad to make your day, Doc.

In addition to the four days in the hospital I was out of my practice for several weeks. Upon returning, I could see only one or two patients a day. I still had pain and a limited range of motion, but worse than that, I had shaking in my right hand, my working hand. For a dentist, this is equivalent to losing your pitching hand.

The shaking, combined with the posttraumatic stress disorder I suffered from the accident, devastated my dental practice. I was forced to do everything much more slowly. This frustrated my dental staff because each procedure took so long to complete. My patients, too, were not happy. My family suffered because I was always late getting home. Nobody understood how hard it had become to do even the simplest of things, like shaving or getting dressed. In fact, just buttoning my shirt had become as difficult as cycling up a steep hill.

I understood that I was headed toward financial disaster.

The shaking was diagnosed as benign essential familial tremor (when you hear four terms for a medical condition it can be translated as: we-don't know-what the heck-this is). The only treatment option available was deep brain stimulation. Brain surgery goes against one of my rules: I do not want anyone fondling my brains. As Woody Allen once said, "Not my brain, that's my second favorite organ!" So here I was, Mr. Positive Thinker, Mr. Motivational Speaker, and I had lost my usual optimism. I slipped into a deep clinical depression. Not only had I crashed physically and financially, I now had crashed spiritually. I had no gratitude and no purpose, and every response I chose was ordinary…at best!

I began simply walking through the motions of life. I felt like a failure and nothing could stop me from feeling the dark cloud of depression. All I could think was: " Why me? Why me? Why me?" I needed help. I needed professional help.

I will always have gratitude to our two best friends for the gift that they gave to me. They set me up with a psychologist. Although this might sound corny, I will call her Hope, for she taught me the importance of having hope. She was a survivor of the Holocaust, and she brought with her tremendous depth, intelligence, scientific and spiritual knowledge, as well as a message of hope and the gift of her powerful love. Hope brought me back from the edge. She taught me that I could have hope once again.

Hope is seeing a path to a better future with honesty about present problems.

Hope is the ability to see God's messengers all around you, ready to help you if needed.

She shared with me her story, of the miracle of her survival. When she was 13 years old, she worked for the Rotterdam underground fighting the Nazis. One day an SS officer came to get her as her name was on his list. As she slept upstairs, her father pleaded for her life. "Take me," he said. But the officer said it was her name that was on the list, he could take no one else. They woke her up, and when she saw the SS man she was about to say, "You have Jack." Jack was the head of the underground. She assumed that they must have captured him, as he was hiding in her building. He must have given them her name.

As she was about to speak his name, she felt a "hand" on her mouth. She said nothing. At the last minute, when she was about to leave, her father offered the SS man a Havana cigar in exchange for Hope's life. The SS man took it and crossed off her name.

Because of her miracle, an invisible hand over her mouth, because of her "messenger," she sits with me at each session and offers me my miracle. She transformed my physical and spiritual crash and depression into a messenger. What was my message?

She revealed that message in one of our sessions. At the end of the previous session I had given her a tape of one of my presentations. Before we started the new session, she held the tape in her hand, placed it in front of me on a table, and said, "Now I'm not supposed to say this - you *must quit your day job!* You are an excellent speaker. The tape is amazing! Your shaking is a message to switch from clinical dentistry to full time speaking."

"God is sending you messengers to quit your day job. In your case, it's the accident, the financial woes, the shaking, and the depression itself; they are all messengers to quit your day job." From then on, our goal was to "extract" me from clinical dentistry and start a speaking business. And we did it! I am now a speaker and author.

So, Why Me?
Why Me? So That... I could learn to recognize God's messengers.
Why Me? So That... I could learn to listen for my message.
Why Me? So That... I could learn my path to happiness.
Why Me? So That... I could write this book and help you discover *Your Path to Happiness.*

With this in mind, I look to my suffering as a blessing; I have gratitude.

If not for the accident and my Parkinson's disease, I would not have had time to write this book. I would be busy in my dental office making that sound of the dental drill. You may not like that sound, but that baby is music to my ears! Yes, I loved doing dentistry, but I love speaking and writing even more. Without my accident, I never would've realized this. As a doctor of dentistry, I was simply healing a person physically. As The Values Doctor, I can heal another person's soul. I am connecting to their innermost light. Using the healing power of values, I am helping people overcome challenges on their path to happiness. How cool is that? I was able to use many of the tools I learned from my experiences to sell my practice, get out of financial difficulty, and begin my speaking business. I now do dental and motivational speaking all around the world. And get this… people pay me to talk! What a miracle!

After selling the practice, I was diagnosed with Parkinson's disease. Great! Great?

What's so great about having a degenerative disease that, over time, will cripple me, and put me into a wheelchair, and make it hard to walk and talk? I'm happy? You bet. I now look for a reason to be happy. I look for the Light. I look for purpose and meaning in everything that happens to me in everything I do. Remember that with my earlier diagnosis of benign essential familial tremor, my only option was to have deep brain stimulation. Now, with a diagnosis of Parkinson's disease, there is no need for brain surgery yet. I have many therapies available. What a blessing! All the suffering I had with the accident, as well as four years of shaking and a bleak diagnosis, was so that I could have gratitude with the diagnosis of Parkinson's disease.

People often expect me to talk and write much more in the way of details about my Parkinson's disease. I will discuss it a bit right now and give some details further in the book. However, I find that it's not that important at this point. The medicines are working well, and I have hope that there will be a cure before my condition becomes much worse. Even if

I never get *cured*, I have had significant *healing*. I do not feel that I'm suffering from a disease. I am simply living with my messenger and learning many messages. I am on my path to happiness, and I am very thankful for its blessings.

I am grateful for Parkinson's as it has kept me connected to the healing power of values.

I am grateful for Parkinson's as it has kept me thinking and acting on purpose.

I am grateful for Parkinson's as it has taught me how to be *responsible* and solve many problems.

I am grateful for Parkinson's, as it has taught me not to complain or blame others.

I am grateful for Parkinson's, as it reminds me that, although I have problems, many live with problems far worse than mine.

I am grateful for Parkinson's, as it has motivated me to uncover the principles and tools that I will show you in the pages of this book. Those principles are the framework for *Your Path to Happiness.*

I am grateful for Parkinson's as it helps me to *be* happy, while on my path to *becoming* someone who achieves happiness.

How about you? **Why you?**

Think back over your life. What stories in your life have taught you important lessons? What messengers have been sent your way with important messages for you? How do these stories help you answer your questions?

+ "Why me?" Why do I suffer from pain and problems?
+ "Why me?" What is the purpose of my existence? What value do I add to the world?
+ "Why me?" What is the purpose of my work? What value do I add through my work?

Answering these questions is an essential part of *Your Path to Happiness*. Happiness requires thinking and acting on purpose. Thinking is all about asking and answering questions. The better the questions, the better the answers we will get. We must then learn how to act based on those answers. That is acting on purpose.

Let's begin with an exercise that I have used with people in business. While it was first used in a business training setting, it applies to all of us. We are all in "business". We are in the business of life. We all do something. At the very least we breathe, and we may even eat (Okay, I admit it, I'm good at eating). We are husbands and wives. We are moms and dads. We are students. We are readers, artists, TV viewers, movie viewers, and sports fans. I think you get the idea. We all "work". The exercise consists of a series of questions and answers. We will explore these questions throughout the book. Please take the time to ask yourself these questions and write the answers. It is the first step on *Your Path to Happiness.*

Why Do You Work Here?

You are a unique creation. Never in the history of the universe has there ever been another you. You were created to do something special, to contribute in some unique way, to add some specific value to this world. If so, why have you chosen to work where you do? (Remember that when I use the term work, I mean whatever you do most of the time. That includes childcare, volunteering, etc.) Why have you chosen to work where you do? You are an independent corporation. Debbie Inc. You could give your services anywhere. Why do you work here? This is the first step in lighting the way for you to understand how you have come to be who you are today. To achieve a higher future level of happiness, you must start from where you are today. How can you find the answer? Using *Your Path to Happiness,* you must take a journey. You must take *your* journey.

WHY DO YOU WORK HERE?

* Where do you work?

  _____

* What do you do there?

  _____

* Why did you choose to work there?

  _____

* Do you plan to keep working there? (Elaborate.)

  _____

* What do you enjoy most about working there?

  _____

* What do you enjoy least about working there?

  _____

* In what way is working there meaningful?

  _____

* In what way does working there help you fulfill your purpose in life?

  _____

* If you won the lottery and had all the money you needed, would you still work there?

  _____

* If yes/no, why?

  _____

  _____

  _____

* What do your answers to these questions tell you about your work, your purpose, and your happiness today?

  _____

  _____

  _____

To understand what these answers mean, and to continue on this journey, you must ask more questions. The next question is…

Why Do You Work?

What is the purpose of work? Why do any work? How do you benefit? There are two reasons to work. **Reason #1 is to make money**. We need money to meet our needs. We need it for clothing and shelter. We need it for acquiring the things we need and desire. Let's be honest, we all need money. That's a good thing, so long as it has been acquired ethically. But money is always to be used as a means toward some end. We must take care never to value money as an end in itself. That is when we get into trouble with money. Money has trade value, but it does not give or reflect your personal value. You are valuable and unique unrelated to your money.

If money helps us to get what we want, then what is it that we want? Here we can find the second reason for working. **Reason #2 is to give our lives meaning and purpose**. It is certainly true that we are physical beings with physical needs. We are also spiritual beings with spiritual needs. For us to be successful and happy, we must be living a life with meaning. Work is the activity that actualizes our need for meaning. That is why it is so important to do work that is meaningful to you. Work must help you meet your purpose in life. Many people die soon after retirement, because they think they have lost their purpose for living.

So which is more important, money or meaning? The first answer is yes! Both are important and are bound to one another in a state of paradox. No money, no mission. No mission, no meaning. We need money to enable us to do that which we value. In business, we need money to produce goods; to market, sell, and distribute those goods; to research and develop newer and better goods; and to pay employees and ourselves. Without money there is no business and thus no mission, no purpose. However, a business whose focus is only on money will not be a source of deep meaning for those who work there. People need a mission that gives purpose and meaning to their lives. In your productive life, there should be meaning, because that is where you spend so much of your time. The majority of your time needs to be on purpose in order for you to build happiness in your life. The same is true in our personal lives. If we focus only on money, without doing that which we find meaningful and of value, our lives will be incomplete.

No money, no mission. No mission, no meaning. That is the paradox of life at work and at home. It is not either/or, it is *and*. We need both. Although we need both, we need them in the proper balance. Ultimately, meaning is more important than money. Money is only a means toward other ends. Money is not valuable in and of itself. Meaning, however, is valuable in and of itself. We are on this planet to make meaning in our life far more than we are here to make money in our life. The trick is to balance:

- our need for money with our need for meaning
- our physical needs with our spiritual needs
- our needs at work with our needs at home

How are we to find that balance? How are we to know how to both make money and find meaning? What is it that gives life meaning? Meaning comes from finding our purpose by connecting to timeless values. How does meaning connect to purpose and values? We will learn about that in the following chapters. We will begin our search for balance with a story about my son.

My son is a man whom I deeply respect. When it came time for college, he had been accepted in the University Of Illinois College Of Business, which at the time was ranked as the number five business school in the country. He has an amazing knowledge of computers, and had created his own business of computer networking and troubleshooting, which helped fund his activities throughout high school. It seemed to be a natural path. It was something he enjoyed, something for which he had talent, and something that would create a career that could support him financially. After one semester he came to my wife and me and told us that he wanted to switch out of the College of Business and into the College of Fine and Applied Arts. Instead of a career in business, he wanted to be an actor. He wanted to give up a career that could be lucrative for one that most likely would not.

Now here's the problem of preaching to your family: sometimes they listen! He said, "Dad, I have to do what's deep inside me, what I believe is my purpose. I don't want to spend my time wishing I was doing something else or be so busy doing "my job" that there is little time left for what I truly enjoy. I see adults all around me who are in jobs that they don't really love. I don't want that to fill my life. People try things and fail and start over many times. If I fail as an actor, I will just start again and do something else. But if I never try to do what I feel is my purpose, then I truly will have failed." How do you argue with that?

He did switch schools, graduated with high honors and has been gainfully employed since he graduated. He is following his purpose and is on his path to happiness.

WHY DO YOU WORK?

✦ How did you come to work where you do now?

_____

_____

✦ Ask yourself — was it for money or meaning, neither or both? (Elaborate)

_____

_____

✦ What do you enjoy doing?

_____

_____

✦ What are you good at doing?

_____

_____

✦ What activities or jobs do you find meaningful?

_____

_____

✦ If you won the lottery and had all the money you needed, would you still work at all?

_____

_____

✦ If yes/no, why?

_____

_____

✦ What do your answers to these questions tell you about your purpose in working?

_____

_____

_____

_____

This leads us to the next question:

WHY DO YOU?

Why do you exist? Why were you put here on this earth? What is your mission? What is your USP?

In business, USP usually stands for Unique Selling Proposition. In this book we will focus on two other versions of USP. First USP = your Unique and Special Purpose? Second, USP = your Unique and Special Path. Before you can know why you work and choose the right work for you, you must know why you are here. You must know your purpose in life. You must know what you value, what gives you meaning. What is it that you enjoy doing and are very good at doing? Discovering your mission here on earth is difficult but essential. We will do a worksheet in Chapter 6 on this question. How will knowing values, meaning, and purpose lead to happiness? What about thinking and acting on purpose? Clearly we need to ask more questions. The next question is...

WHY YOU?

This is where we started. When phrased this way the implication is why do you suffer from problems and pain. How can we experience happiness in the presence of challenges, obstacles, pain and problems? We must find our purpose. However, to find our purpose requires asking a final question…

WHY?

Why? Now we have come to the ultimate question. Why? Why does *anything* exist? Why is there a Universe? Why are there planets? Why are there human beings? Why are there problems? Why is there suffering and pain? Why are there laws of nature? Why is there beauty? Why is there love? Why is there life? What does it all mean? Why do we ask why?

We ask why because we are human beings. We have these questions deep inside of us. As we said earlier, they come to us from a part of us that is beyond our bodies and even beyond our minds. These questions come to us not from the physical, but from the metaphysical (literally beyond the physical). These questions come from our souls. Our souls yearn for reconnection, to become whole again. Our job as human beings is to reconnect our souls to that Power & Loving Greater Than Ourselves.

How can you connect to the Light, to the Power & Loving Greater Than Ourselves, the source of messengers who answer those questions and the source of messengers of happiness? How can you achieve happiness at work and at home? In the next few chapters we will try to answer these questions.

Before I can "enlighten" you with some answers to these questions, I need to empower you with two more Path Prescriptions from *Your Path to Happiness*, one each in the next two chapters. Then we will focus on achieving happiness in Chapter 4.

Remember from the introduction that Prescription #1 is "Using Timeless Values for Thinking and Acting on Purpose." The next two prescriptions are tools to get you thinking on purpose. Path Prescription #2 is "The Lessons of Learning." Path Prescription #3 is "The Universal Whole-Parts-Whole Process." These prescriptions help you to Light *Your Path to Happiness*. Light is a conduit between the physical and metaphysical world. Light represents enlightenment and understanding, and can reveal the source of thinking on purpose. The Lessons of Learning is a tool revealing both the limits and the power of human learning. Any time you need to answer a question or learn something new, this powerful prescription will be helpful for you. It is a tool that is especially relevant for finding your purpose, a key step along *Your Path to Happiness*.

The Universal Whole-Parts-Whole Process helps you understand the source of the lessons of learning and find your purpose. At the same time it helps you to understand the source of pain and problems, as well as how to find solutions to those problems. Finally, it is my source for *Your Path to Happiness* itself. Sounds interesting? Let's move on.

Path Principles

- ✦ Why me: So That…

- ✦ Hope is seeing a path to a better future with honesty about present problems.

- ✦ Hope is the ability to see God's messengers all around you, ready to help you if needed.

- ✦ Having gratitude helps me to *be* happy, while on my path to *becoming* someone who achieves happiness.

- ✦ Why do you work here?
  - ✦ Money
  - ✦ & Meaning (USP)

— CHAPTER 2: —
"WHY ME?"… "SO THAT___!"

Path Prescription #2: The Lessons of Learning

After my bike accident, I was constantly asking myself, "Why me?" Why do I suffer from problems? I wanted happiness. My problems were preventing me from having happiness. I was looking for answers, for enlightenment, and for understanding. I was in search of a **Light** to guide me on a path of learning. It was then that I discovered the lessons of learning. Not only do the lessons help answer my question "Why me?"—they can be used to help answer any deep questions.

Lesson of Learning #1: Why me? I will never know for sure.
Absolute truth exists, but we will never know it absolutely.

Absolute truth exists. There exists within each of us a fundamental consciousness that **the universe makes sense**. We believe it can be understood. It is this sense deep within us that the universe makes sense that is shared by both the spiritualist and the scientist. While each one has a different concept of how the universe makes sense or what the "meaning" of existence might be, both share the belief that, somehow, everything makes sense in the end. This is a pure and simple belief. It is an assumption. There is no ultimate rational reason for this actually to be true.

Absolute truth exists, but we will never know it absolutely. Only God knows for sure. This is the essence of Lesson #1. As Rabbi Lawrence Kushner has said, "The first commandment is: I'm God. The second commandment is: You're not!"[4] In other words, as much as people would like to believe that they can understand everything, that ability is reserved for God alone. Absolute truth, the sacred, exists, but is hidden from us. We cannot completely fathom what God thinks. To paraphrase Rabbi Bachya: Just as it is impossible to explain the concept of fire to a fish, so it is impossible for us to understand God and the metaphysical.[5]

Socrates, on trial for his life, stated, "God only is wise."[6] When the Athenian Divine Oracle revealed that there was no man wiser than Socrates, Socrates understood this to mean that human wisdom is worth nothing. Socrates is wise because he understands lesson one. He **knows** that he **cannot know** (notice the paradox). True wisdom is the knowledge that we cannot know anything *for sure*. We will never be able to make complete, perfect, and absolute sense out of our own existence.

Therefore, if I want to understand why suffering exists, I must first understand that I will never know for sure. That is the human condition— **uncertainty**. The desire for explanations is thus a very understandable human need. We want to hear **The Truth** and we want to understand why and for what purpose a certain thing happened. Our expectation is that this truth should be easily understood. It is based on our deepest belief: that the universe makes sense. We forget that we are not God. God is infinite. Infinity is boundless; there is no boundary to God's knowledge. We are finite, limited in our knowledge. While absolute truth exists, we will never know it absolutely. This is one of the primordial sources of our pain. Deep inside us is the belief that life should make sense. We should be able to answer all our questions with certainty. The fact that we must live with significant uncertainty, especially regarding life's deepest questions and life's greatest problems, is the source of significant pain and suffering. It is an obstacle to happiness.

Along with uncertainty regarding suffering comes pluralism, the idea that there are many potentially correct views. Since we cannot know for sure which of the many views is in fact correct, we must choose between two or more of these imperfect choices. We could choose incorrectly. We could make a mistake. Mistakes cause more problems and pain.

Notice, however, that my human freedom, choice, also comes from my human limitations of uncertainty and pluralism. As I said, since we cannot know for sure which of the many views is in fact correct, and since uncertainty exists, we are free to make choices. Uncertainty leads us to either pain and problems or freedom of choice. Unfortunately, our brains are wired such that we can only recognize one of these two human attributes at a time. Inner peace, happiness, is highly dependent on which one of the two attributes— freedom or problems— we choose to emphasize. Too often we only focus on our human limitation. We are stressed and we suffer in many circumstances because we cannot know for sure why any particular circumstance exists and what we should do about it. We become overwhelmed and ask God questions. We ask questions for which the answers are often hidden from us. And so our stress and suffering increases.

However, along with this great burden of stress and suffering comes the great blessing of choice. We have freedom. Emerging from the darkness of uncertainty itself is the power to choose a response to any condition in which we find ourselves. We can find meaning in suffering. If life is meaningful, and suffering is a part of life, then suffering can be meaningful. If I focus on my freedom as opposed to my limitations, then I am a step closer to inner peace.

Once, when I was at the Israeli Holocaust Museum Yad Vashem, I spoke with one of the guides who told me a story about his grandfather.

It was winter and his grandfather had not eaten for several days. When walking down the street, two

German soldiers came up to him. He figured that they would probably shoot him, and he would die right then and there. One of the soldiers asked him how long had it been since he had eaten. He replied that it had been several days. To his complete surprise, the soldier took out a loaf of bread and handed it to him. The soldier asked his buddy if he had some chocolates. His buddy said, "Sure," and handed them over to the grandfather.

Each time my guide's grandfather told this story, he reminded his grandson that **everyone always has a choice**.

These Germans chose better than most. They chose an extraordinary response for those conditions. What is your extraordinary response to your conditions?

Do you focus on the pain of problems or the freedom of choice? If you focus on the freedom of choice, you are then free to move on to lesson #2.

So, Lesson #1 - Why me? I will never know for sure. But I have **Freedom**.

Lesson of Learning #2: Why Me? I want to know anyway.
To be perfectly human is to know imperfectly.

While lesson one reveals that we will never know for sure, lesson two proclaims: I don't care, I want to know anyway! Although perfect knowledge is impossible, significant knowledge is attainable. We live with imperfect truth, uncertain truth, human truth. Lesson number two proposes: That's okay! Even though human truth is always flawed, it is nonetheless substantial truth.

In the presence of uncertainty, I still believe deeply in the concept that this universe makes sense. I want to understand, even if imperfectly, the structure, meaning, purpose, and value of life, and then live by that understanding. Life becomes a quest in search of how to think and act in the most sensible way possible. Science and spirituality are tools in that quest. Science can help us understand the structure and functioning of our awesome universe. Science has predictive power and can give us some level of control over our world. However, it cannot tell us about values, meaning, and purpose. That is the role of spirituality. Spirituality can connect us to the infinite Power and Loving Greater Than Ourselves—the source of timeless values, meaning, and purpose.

Robert Kane, in his tape for the Teaching Company titled *The Quest for Meaning, Values, Ethics and the Modern Experience*, quotes the Greek philosopher Xenophanes:

> *"The gods did not reveal from the beginning*
> *All things to us; but in the course of time*

Through seeking, men found that which is better.
But as for certain truth, no man has known it,
Nor will he know it; neither of the gods,
Nor yet of all the things of which I speak.
And even if by chance he were to utter
The final truth, he would himself not know it;
For all is but a woven web of guesses."[7]

We aspire to know and to learn, even though we will never know for sure. Our lives become a quest for greater knowledge. On that journey, however, while we are alive, we never fully arrive. Learning is a quest for physical and spiritual growth. Life is a heroic quest, an epic journey, my path, and my story. **I'm not only a human being I am also a human becoming**.

Kane calls this quest a search in the realm of aspiration.[8] He points out that aspiration comes from the Latin term "aspirare" which means to breathe forth. Our spirit breathes forth in search of knowledge. We aspire to know the truth with the requirement that we can never know with certainty that we have attained the goal. We seek those truths that represent ultimate values, the meaning, and purpose of life, and then we strive to live such a life. I can't know for sure "Why me?" but I can stay on the path of searching for an answer. I can spend the rest of my life seeking and aspiring to know. The quest for answers to life's hard questions is the first step on a sacred path, our Sacred Path of Serving Others. What is a sacred path?

+ A sacred journey is a quest for meaning on the path of life.
+ Buddhists speak of the Noble Eightfold Path or Way.
+ Confucianism and Taoism have a central notion called the Tao, literally the "Way". This term implies both the way of the universe and the way for humans to live.
+ Hindu tradition speaks of different yogas (of knowledge, devotion, works, or meditation), literally disciplines, or paths, toward liberation.
+ Jesus said: "I am the Way, the Life, and the Truth."
+ In Judaism the legal code is called the Halachah or the Path.
+ Similarly, in Islam, Muslim law is Shariah, which literally means the "right path."

The lifelong quest for inner peace, for happiness, begins on this path in search of knowledge and proper behavior. It is the first step along *Your Path to Happiness*. I will never know for sure why my accident happened. But seeking to know anyhow jump-started my personal quest for inner peace, which in and of itself has given me purpose. We will see how important my purpose is to my happiness.

Travel along this path is fueled by responsibility. We are responsible. As Stephen Covey explains: "Look at the word responsibility— 'response-ability'—the ability to choose your response."[9] Responsibility is also our ability to respond in the presence of uncertainty. It is my human responsibility to answer life's questions and live by those answers. Even though I cannot know for sure whether my choices are right or wrong, I am still responsible. I must decide for myself, and you must decide for yourself and choose your path through life.

Rabbi Tarfon said, "It is not up to you to finish the job, but you are not free from doing some of the work."[10] I must accept accountability and responsibility. Responsibility is the ability to respond extraordinarily in the face of uncertainty. It is my response to my God-given abilities.

There are two parts to responsibility. 1) The ability to respond using my freedom, even with uncertainty. 2) Choosing a positive, ethical, and moral response. Acting as one ought to act. In other words your responsibility is to:

Search for truth & Do the right thing.

Think & Act on Purpose.

Viktor Frankl was a psychiatrist who survived Auschwitz. He was asked if there was freedom in a concentration camp. In his book, *Man's Search for Meaning,* Frankl says, "To be sure, a human being is a finite thing, and his freedom is restricted. It is not freedom from conditions, but it is freedom to take a stand toward the conditions."[11] In other words, we are not free to choose our conditions. However, we are completely free to choose our response to those conditions. You can accept what is and choose your extraordinary response. Be responsible. **Responsibility is the name of the human game.**

The Israeli violinist Yitzhak Perlman contracted polio at the age of four. Ever since, he has had to wear metal braces on his legs and walk with crutches; yet he became one of the great virtuosi of our time. On one occasion, the story is told, he came out onto the stage at a concert to play a violin Concerto. Laying down his crutches, he placed the violin under his chin and began tuning the instrument when, with an audible crack, one of the strings broke. The audience expected him to send for another string, but instead he signaled the conductor to begin, and he proceeded to play the Concerto entirely on three strings. At the end of the performance, the audience gave him a standing ovation and called on him to speak. What he said, according to the story, was this: "**Our task is to make music with what remains.**"

This referred as much to his polio as to his violin. He responsibly accepted what was, and to both his polio and his music he chose an extraordinary response.

Lesson #1 - Why me? I will never know for sure. But I have **Freedom**.
Lesson #2 - Why me? I want to know anyway. I have **Responsibility.**
Lesson of Learning #3: **Why me? I want to know my purpose.**

Why do I exist? What is my purpose in life?

If you accept the notion that our existence makes some sense, then how do you make sense of your life—your existence? In other words, what is your purpose? What music were you put here to make? Make sure that, when it is time for you to leave this world, you do not go with most of your music still in you. Do not focus on how hard it is to play your music. Focus instead on the success and happiness your music can bring you.

Once there was a traveler who came upon three individuals working with stone. Curious as to what the workers were doing with the stones, the traveler approached the first worker and asked, "What are you doing with these stones?" The worker responded, "I am a stonecutter and I am cutting stones. Day after day after day I come here and I just cut stones. That's why they call me a stonecutter." The traveler approached the second worker and asked, "What are you doing with these stones?" The second worker explained, "I am a stonecutter and although the work is hard, I am trying to make enough money to support my family. I love my family and am willing to work hard for them. That's why they call me a stonecutter." The traveler made his way to the third worker and asked, "What are you doing with these stones?" With a beaming smile on his face the third worker declared, "I am a stonecutter and I am building a cathedral. It is my passion in life to use my artistic talents to build this cathedral to God's glory and to inspire people. My father worked on this cathedral, I am working on this cathedral, and it probably will not be completed until my son's generation. I love what I do. That's why they call me a stonecutter."

Now, the question is which kind of stonecutter are you? Are you the kind that simply goes about your daily tasks moaning, groaning and complaining? Or are you the kind that performs your duties for the money but not the mission? Or, finally, are you the kind that sees the bigger picture and has found a higher purpose to all you do?

Lesson #1 - Why me? I will never know for sure. But I have **Freedom**.

Lesson #2 - Why me? I want to know anyway. I have **Responsibility.**

Lesson #3 - Why me? I want to know my purpose. I have a **Purpose.**

In Summary:

Lesson of Learning #1: Why me? I will never know for sure. Absolute truth exists, but we will never know it absolutely. Uncertainty and pluralism exists, but I have **Freedom.**

Lesson of Learning #2: Why Me? I want to know anyway. To be perfectly human is to know imperfectly. I search for truth and do the right thing, I take **Responsibility.**

Lesson of Learning #3: Why me? I want to know my purpose.
Why do I exist? What is my purpose in life? Always connect any answer to your **Purpose.**

Freedom, Responsibility, and Purpose

Those are the values that we learn from the three lessons of learning.

Lesson #1: In the presence of UNCERTAINTY:
We can choose to focus on problems or freedom.
The extraordinary response is to **choose freedom.**

Lesson #2: In the presence of OUR FREEDOM:
We can choose responsibility or blame.
The extraordinary response is to **choose responsibility.**

Lesson #3: In the presence of PROBLEMS AND PAIN:
We can choose to focus on problems or purpose.
The extraordinary response is to **choose purpose.**

Freedom, Responsibility and Purpose are the values that empower choosing a response that is extraordinary.

The Lessons of Learning teach us that there are two responses to problems and pain. The **ordinary response** to problems and pain is to ask "Why me?— and answer:"because____."

You want to fill in the blank with blame. You are focusing on your problems and your pain. If you can blame it on someone or something then it's not your fault, you are not responsible. Blame makes you feel better. But it doesn't solve your problems. It turns you into a victim. This doesn't get you anywhere.

You must change your thinking.

Using ordinary thinking you answer "Why me?" with **"because ___,"**
The **extraordinary response** to "Why me?" is:
"So that___!"

You fill in the blank with something extraordinary, something purposeful, something of meaning, and something of ultimate timeless value. By changing your thinking and your answer, you have also changed the question itself.

Instead of asking *the ordinary question,* **"Why do I suffer?"** You are now asking *the extraordinary question,* **"Why do I exist?"**

You ask, "Why me? Why do I exist?" and you answer "**So that** you can discover your purpose and actualize it in your life!

You are here on this earth to do something special, something extraordinary. You are here to add some value to the universe.

Now here comes the key point of these lessons:

In life you can choose to focus on *Problems* or *Purpose.* Focusing on *Problems* causes pain and suffering. However, when you focus on *Purpose,* then:
The Power of Purpose Overrides the Pain of Problems!

The *Power of Purpose*, your "So that___!" can override the pain of any problems.

Pain and problems exist **So that** you can solve those problems and heal that suffering. Our purpose is to solve our own and each other's problems, leading to extraordinary levels of success and happiness.

> **Purpose is the flipside of problems.**
> **Without problems you would have no purpose.**

Without patients with dental problems, I could not fulfill my purpose as a dentist. Without customers or clients with problems, you could not fulfill your purpose as a professional. I have problems so that you can help me; you have problems so that I can help you.

Why me? So That... So That I can help solve problems.

What problems were you put here to solve? What problems do you face at work and at home? Your purpose is to solve those problems on your own or with the help and expertise of others. What problems do others face at your work and your home? Your purpose is to help them solve their problems with your expertise. You need to *expect problems*, since solving them is your purpose. Your problems themselves are messengers with the message: Stay on purpose.

The power of your purpose overrides the pain of your problems. That's the secret to *Your Path to Happiness*. Nietzsche said, "He who has a meaningful *why* to live for can bear with almost any *how*."[12] Purpose is what gives every action of your life meaning. Without purpose, you are without meaningful focus. Acting on purpose is what leads to happiness. We will elaborate on this later. Every action that you take should be on purpose. If you do not have a purpose, you must find one. Once you have found one you must learn to stay on purpose.

My mother has a value of family togetherness on Jewish holidays that acts like an electromagnet on her children and grandchildren. This value is part of her purpose of being a loving mother in a close family. In Judaism, the most important holiday is the weekly Sabbath. Our Sabbath begins on Friday evening and ends 25 hours later on Saturday night. A few years ago, she had open heart surgery on a Monday morning. Most people would spend at least a week in the hospital leaving on the next Monday or Tuesday, if not even later. Before going into surgery, my mother announced to us all that she was going home Friday afternoon for the Sabbath. Her doctor said it is possible, but highly unlikely. Knowing our mother, we made arrangements for her to spend the Sabbath at home.

After the surgery on Monday morning, she was avoiding taking any morphine by Monday afternoon! That's open heart surgery, with tubes in her chest, and post surgical pain, and no morphine to help. Why not use the morphine?

Morphine slows healing and her ability to get off the respirator and have the tubes removed. The longer she was on the respirator and the tubes were in her, the longer she would have to stay in the hospital. Her purpose was to be home Friday afternoon, so bye-bye morphine. Imagine the pain that she experienced! All week she forced herself to do all the things necessary to get home Friday afternoon. On Friday morning, the doctor told her he was totally amazed at her progress. He had rarely seen anything like it. She was discharged Friday afternoon and home she went to her well deserved Sabbath with her family.

This is a great example that *The Power of Purpose Overrides the Pain of Problems.* My mother's purpose, her "So That___!" overrode the pain of her problems. **So that** she could be together with her family on the Sabbath she endured the pain and overcame hardships necessary to be discharged Friday. She experienced much happiness on that Sabbath. Having a purpose was the key.

Staying on purpose can lead to happiness. Purpose itself can be found in the realm of the higher Light in the dimension of timeless values. Purpose can then bring that Light into our daily lives. Using the values from the lessons of learning— Freedom, Responsibility and Purpose—you can learn to think and act on purpose. You can experience happiness.

In our search for Light, for enlightenment, for answers

to difficult questions, the lessons of learning is a powerful tool. However, we need to know how to get access to that hidden dimension where healing values and our own unique purpose can be found. Furthermore we still need to understand more deeply the source of problems and their solutions. We need to understand the source of uncertainty, of pain, and of healing. We need to understand more about thinking and acting on purpose and how it relates to *Your Path to Happiness*. That will require Path Prescription #3: The Universal Whole-Parts-Whole Process.

Path Principles

- **Lesson of Learning #1: Why me? I will never know for sure.**
  - Absolute truth exists, but we will never know it absolutely.
  - Uncertainty and pluralism exists, but I have **Freedom.**
- **Lesson of Learning #2: Why Me? I want to know anyway.**
  - To be perfectly human is to know imperfectly.
  - I search for truth & do the right thing, I take **Responsibility.**
- **Lesson of Learning #3: Why me? I want to know my purpose.**
  - Why do I exist? What is my purpose in life?
  - Always connect any answer to your **Purpose.**
- "Why me?" The ordinary response is "Because ____."
- "Why me?" The extraordinary response is "So That___!"
- The power of purpose overrides the pain of problems.
- Purpose is the flipside of problems.
- Without problems you would have no purpose.
- "Why me?" So That I can help you solve problems!

— CHAPTER 3: —
THE SOURCE OF PROBLEMS
AND SOLUTIONS

Path Prescription #3: The Universal Whole-Parts-Whole Process.

We remain with the following questions: What are the sources of uncertainty, problems, and pain? In the presence of these issues, how can we heal and achieve happiness?

For me, paradoxically, the most rational answers to these questions can be found in Jewish mysticism, the Kabbalah. Before we discuss the Kabbalah, we must understand the *Universal Whole-Parts-Whole Process*. In this process, the universe initially exists as a whole and breaks or is broken into its parts, followed by the attempt to reconstruct the parts back together as a whole.

For example, one can start with a watch. Let us say that the watch stops working properly. Something inside the watch has broken. The watch is no longer working as a whole. There is a broken part. We've gone from whole to parts (whole→parts). What we do next is try to fix the parts and reconnect it to the whole (parts→whole). If we can do that, we are back to a whole, functioning watch. The process is thus:

Whole→Parts→Whole

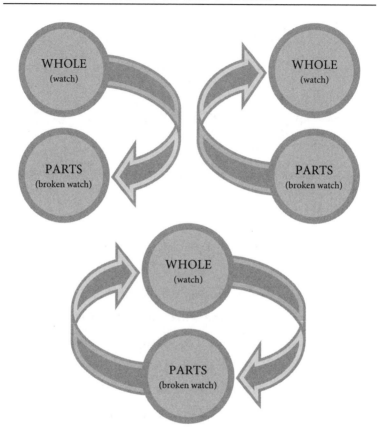

Another example of the whole-parts-whole process is the scientific method. You begin with all of nature, whole and complete. Now you focus on one small part of that whole reality, or ask a question about one small part of reality. You run an experiment and make some observations concerning one part. For example, let's say you take some of your blood and look at it under a microscope. You've gone from whole to parts (whole→parts). You started with your whole body and blood all in one unified entity. You break up the whole by taking out one part (your blood). You observe and investigate that one part. You now understand that part in a way that was not possible before. Science then takes the new information about the parts and tries to re-integrate those parts, that new knowledge, into the whole of nature—parts back to whole (parts→whole). By understanding the blood and the microscopic elements that make up your blood, we add to our understanding of the whole human body and its processes. The net result again is a process of:

Whole→Parts→Whole

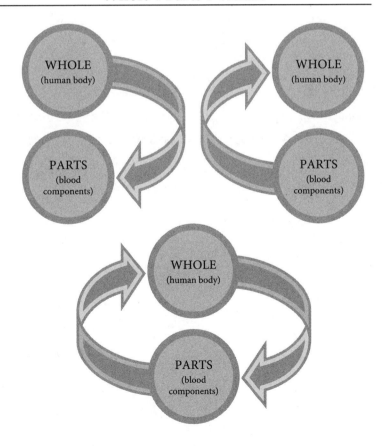

We will study the scientific method in further detail in Chapter 5.

Even our birth and our life follow the whole-parts-whole process. The Power & Loving Greater Than Ourselves, God, exists as the wholeness of everything, the matrix in which everything exists. Rabbi Adin Steinsaltz[13] notes that in the simplicity of the womb we understand this on a primal level. There, we begin life with the experience of undifferentiated wholeness. I exist within that whole, and that whole exists within me (whole). When I am born (whole→parts), I am faced with a myriad of disconnected details (parts), each of which demands to be observed and somehow integrated into my mind. In life, our job is to take the parts, connect them and re-create the whole (parts→whole). Whole-parts-whole is the process of life. As we've learned in the lessons of learning, deep inside us is the belief that the universe makes sense. We believe the details of our experiences can be unified. We seem to have the ability to connect the parts that we experience into some greater whole.

Whole→Parts→Whole

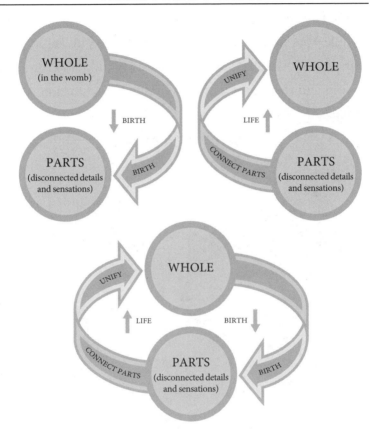

Now we should be able to grasp Rabbi Isaac Luria's amazing understanding of Kabbalah and creation. Before creation, there was a pre-universe existing as one undifferentiated, infinite, unified whole. All that existed was God. The physical and spiritual were one. At some point, in a way that is unfathomable to the human mind, God withdrew from some of the whole of existence (whole→parts). God wanted to perform an act of love and create us and our world. He wanted to make a space for us. To do that, God withdrew (whole→parts). That's the key to the beginning of our universe. God withdrew, so for us he is hidden. Our job is to find and reconnect with the hidden God. Our job is to re-create the whole by reconnecting the parts (parts→whole). That is what I mean by a universal whole-parts-whole process.

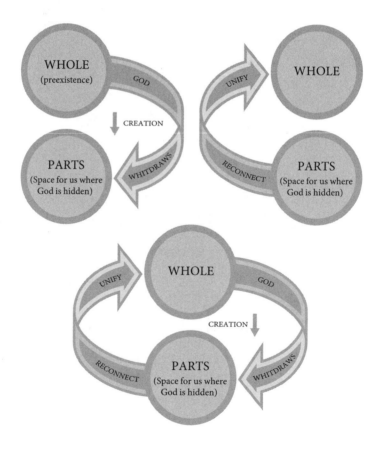

Think about it. If the infinite should withdraw, then what would be left would be finite space. If the timeless should withdraw, then what would be left would be time. In our case, both happened, and we were left with space-time, our universe, our "box."

"Creation" of our universe = our space-time box

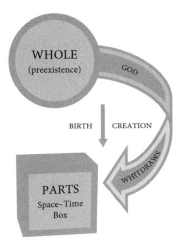

Not only the infinite and timeless withdrew. The Extraordinary (holy) withdrew and what remains is ordinary (secular). The metaphysical (beyond the physical) withdrew leaving the physical universe. Certainty withdrew leaving us in a box of ordinary space-time filled with uncertainty. Through withdrawing, God is now hidden. With God hidden, we have uncertainty, and we cannot know anything for sure. The first lesson of learning operates here. We are separated from God through his withdrawal at creation, or through our birth. We experience the pain of that separation as well as the pain of uncertainty.

To a scientist, our universe, our space-time box (**ST box**), is all there is. It is a closed box. All explanations must come from inside the box itself. There is no need, nor are we allowed, to search for explanations outside of the box, outside of nature. In other words, there can be no supernatural explanations given towards the understanding of the processes of our world and our experiences in it. Our universe is physical. There is no metaphysical. There is nothing beyond the physical. As Laplace answered Napoleon when asked where God was in his concept of the universe, "I have no need for that particular hypothesis."[14] That is the scientific paradigm.

There is a second paradigm. We discussed that paradigm in the introduction. Perhaps our box is not the only dimension. Perhaps, in fact, the box is not completely closed. What if there are hidden openings through which beams of spiritual light can penetrate to us from a higher dimension? What if we can use those openings to connect to that higher dimension? **Spirituality is an awareness of that higher dimension**. Spirituality is the notion that there is more than simply a physical universe, a space-time box. There exists a reality beyond the box that penetrates into the box. The spiritual reality is hidden yet present. With proper awareness, we can perceive its existence and hear the messages that it communicates to those of us in the box. We in the box can, in turn, communicate with that reality out-of-the-box. There can be messengers with messages. That is the greatest difference between the atheist-secularist and religious-spiritualist. Does a Power & Loving Greater Than Ourselves exist in a dimension beyond space-time? The atheists-secularist says no. The religious-spiritualist says yes. I, of course, answer yes. Without such a dimension, I believe there are no absolute truths, no right and wrong, no timeless values, and no objectively meaningful purposes. These could all exist subjectively to us as individuals. I can create my own purpose. I can claim my own values. But these concepts would be personal. Choosing any particular value in any particular situation would be similar to choosing chocolate over vanilla ice cream. Both would be based on personal preferences alone. Without the Power & Loving Greater Than Ourselves, these concepts could not exist objectively, that is to say as objects and as ideas separate from us and our personal perceptions. Also, without the ability to connect to the Power & Loving Greater Than Ourselves, to enter into or have contact with that dimension, we can never know that truth and those timeless values. For all intents and purposes, it would be as if that dimension does not exist.

On a deeper level, Isaiah (45:7) quotes God, "I form the light, and create darkness; I make peace, and create evil." Notice the construction of the sentence. Creation in the Bible means forming something from nothing. God is saying, "I form the light. It is part of me, and I don't need to create it. Darkness, however, requires creation. Darkness is not intrinsically part of me. When I withdraw, when my light is withdrawn, darkness is created. Similarly, I am peace, wholeness and shalom.

I can make peace; it is part of my being. When my peace is withdrawn, evil is created."

Perhaps we can now begin to understand the dilemma facing us today. We live in a world where God is hidden, and hidden along with God are ultimate truths and healing values such as Light, Love, Life, & ShaLom. *We can never be sure that we know anything. As Paul says (1 Corinthians 13:12), "we see through a glass, darkly." We live in "darkness," and it has become possible for us to do evil. We search for light and for peace. We are broken and want to be made whole again. We want to be healed. Without healing, how can we have happiness? That's our journey. That's our quest. We cannot heal; we cannot be made whole again, unless we can connect to timeless healing values in that higher dimension.*

The universe thus began as an undifferentiated whole. God withdrew, which left parts. Before birth, as before creation, there was unity, wholeness. The act of our birth separated us from the total unity. We are now inside our space-time box. **We live in a world of parts, of paradox, of pluralism and uncertainty, creating our pain and problems.**

Whole → Parts

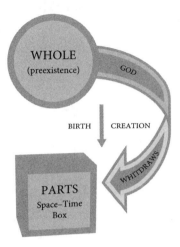

Our goal is to take these separate parts— these challenges, pain, and problems— reconnect them, and once again become whole. This requires a *parts-to-whole process.*

Parts → Whole

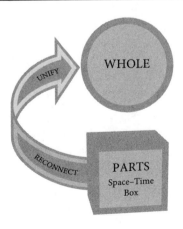

This parts-to-whole portion of the whole-parts-whole process is what I call: **Your Path to Happiness**.

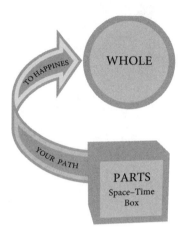

Happiness is achieved by taking the parts and making them whole.

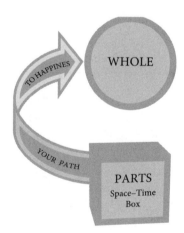

We achieve this happiness through acts of service, acts of love.

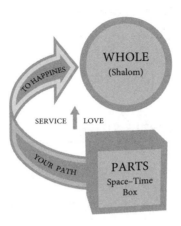

Parts are ordinary. Becoming whole? That is extraordinary. Becoming whole once again through acts of service brings us joy & inner peace—happiness (ShaLom).

To move from parts back to whole, to reconnect, to serve, to unify, and to achieve SHALOM we must:

Solve problems
Heal pain
Address needs   AT WORK   Your Path
Look to satisfy wants   &   ➜   to Happiness
Overcome challenges   AT HOME
Make opportunities

Your Path to Happiness is your journey from parts to whole, from problems to purpose, from pain to healing, from challenges to solutions and from brokenness to shalom.

The process is thus:

Whole→Parts→Whole

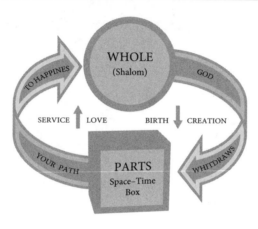

You achieve shalom and happiness by following *Your Path to Happiness*. What, then, is *Your Path to Happiness*?

Your Path to Happiness consists of the following stages:

Whole to Parts Initial Universal Condition: The Setup.

Search for Light: Leaving the ST box and journeying into the spiritual realm.

Timeless Values Connection: Thinking in the metaphysical realm (thinking on purpose).

Act with Love: Returning to the ST box to serve others (acting on purpose).

Create a Life of Holiness: Actualizing values (thinking & acting on purpose).

Seek Moments of ShaLom: Experiencing moments of wholeness, of happiness.

LIGHT LOVE LIFE & SHALOM
IS
YOUR PATH TO HAPPINESS AT WORK & AT HOME

Light	*the source of purpose*	Values
Love	*the purpose*	Virtues
Life	*where the purpose is actualized*	Vocation
ShaLom	*Happiness*	Victory

Joy and inner peace coming
from actualizing purpose

Let's look at the system in detail:

Whole to Parts Initial Universal Condition: The Setup *(Figure 1)*

God—wholeness—withdraws, and we're left with parts, pain, and problems in our ST box. We want to solve our problems and heal our pain. Remember, without this initial condition of pain and problems, you would have no purpose, and you would have no path to happiness. This step sets up *Your Path to Happiness.*

So far the process is the familiar:

Whole→Parts

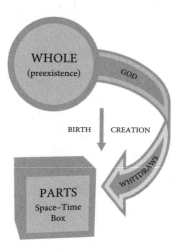

(Figure 1)

Search for Light: Journeying into the spiritual realm. *(Figure 2)*

We want to heal from our pain, problems and challenges. We want to move from parts to whole. We want to reconnect with the Power & Loving Greater Than Ourselves. We search for His light coming from outside our ST box. We temporarily separate from the purely physical, secular, and natural universe and "climb the ladder" into the metaphysical realm. This can be done through prayer, meditation, scriptures, and other tools.

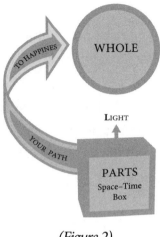

(Figure 2)

Timeless Values Connection: Thinking in the metaphysical realm; Thinking on Purpose.

We connect to the metaphysical light and to the higher values to be found in that dimension. Connect with God's values, holy values, and timeless values. Using those values and your responsibility, search for truth—how you ought to act. You will then act on that truth in your return to the natural universe.

Thinking on Purpose: Seek to discover your purpose using the timeless values found in that dimension. We all have a general human purpose. That purpose is to love–to serve, to reconnect the parts. This can be seen in *Figure 3*. Love, our general purpose, emerges from Light, out of the Timeless Values Connection. We also have a specific, individual purpose. Your purpose is the unique value you add to the universe for which you were created. This is also known as your *primary healing value*. You will use it to heal yourself, and you will use it to heal others at work and at home.

Your healing value, your purpose, is your inner source of happiness. It is your reason for being happy. Connecting with timeless values in the metaphysical realm does give you a sense of wholeness.

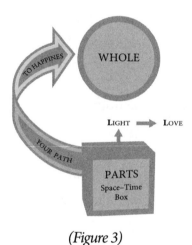

(Figure 3)

Act with Love: Returning to life in the ST box to serve others; Acting on Purpose. *(Figure 4)*

The first act of love is to return to our lives at work and at home. We return to the natural world, our ST box. One is tempted to stay in the metaphysical realm. After all, there is a sense of wholeness here. Why leave? That is a question to which we will soon return. It is a sacrifice, an act of love, an act of service to return to the ST box. We will see the importance of this loving choice. If we do not make this loving choice willingly, we are forced back into the ST box unwillingly.

Acting on Purpose: Once you return to the natural world, base your actions on the values learned in the transcendent realm. Holiness is the process of bringing God's timeless values into your productive daily life. Add value and be of service to yourself and others at work and at home. The guiding principle of service is the Golden Rule.

The power of your purpose overrides the pain of your problems and empowers you to choose to **be happy** no matter what present problems you face.

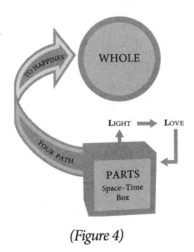

(Figure 4)

Create a Life of Holiness: Actualizing values; Thinking & Acting on Purpose. *(Figure 5)*

Thinking & Acting on Purpose. Now that we have returned

to the ST box, we live our lives inside the box. We actualize our potential within that box. We take ordinary space and time and transform it into the extraordinary. By thinking and acting on purpose along our path through life, we take the secular and transform it into the holy. Life is a journey through **Moments of Encounter**. In those moments, we transform this world from what it is—a place of pain, suffering, and problems—to a place that it ought to be—a place of healing, overcoming challenges, and solving problems. We are God's messengers. Through thinking and acting on purpose, through acts of love and of service, with an attitude of gratitude to God for all of life, we bring God back into the ST box. God dwells within us, within the ST box. We connect to the next stage, shaLom.

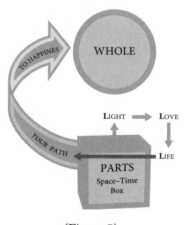

(Figure 5)

Seek Moments of ShaLom:

Moments of wholeness and of happiness. *(Figure 6)*

We can achieve shalom, balanced harmonious unity. Shalom is reaching a level of wholeness. It is the happiness from actualizing *Your Path to Happiness*. Happiness is joy and inner peace. Joy and inner peace are the result of applying the four healing values, Light, Love, Life, & ShaLom, as we just described. Notice in the diagram below how *the process, has transformed and raised the entire ST box* (This can be seen by noting the change of the Life arrowhead position as well as the *Your Path to Happiness* arrow).

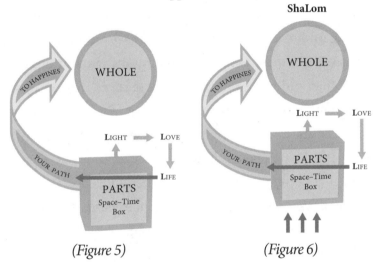

(Figure 5)   *(Figure 6)*

We can experience shalom, wholeness and happiness, but only for moments. Unfortunately, while we're alive, we never fully arrive. We get moments of wholeness, moments of happiness. Life throws new challenges, new problems, and new pain at us.

It is here that entropy enters the game (*Figure 7-8)*. Entropy is the scientific term for random disorder. Any closed system left alone will have an increase in disorder inside that system.

If you closed the door to your teenage child's room and left him inside for one week, upon opening the door you would be presented with a marvelous example of entropy. The same thing is true if you take a garden and never address the weeds. The garden tends toward the wilderness, entropy; the weeds take over. Unless you attend to your business, you know it will fall apart. Entropy is a profound concept when dealing with our universe. Entropy rules every closed system. If our universe box is closed as science proposes, not only is there no metaphysical dimension, but life inside the box is always tending toward disorder. In other words, we are always falling apart. We are, then, always moving toward random disorder rather than order, meaning, or purpose. Even if there was a kind of summit, perhaps inside the box, we could not stay there forever, because inside the box, everything falls apart eventually. Remember, as long as we are alive, we never fully arrive in a permanent state of happiness. Once we overcome one challenge, another one rears its ugly head. That is why, in this life, we only get moments of happiness —moments of shalom. From those moments of shalom and wholeness, we are returned to the ordinary life of parts—the pain, problems and challenges of life in the ST box—of our life at work and at home. Entropy removes the order that we have built using Light, Love, Life, & ShaLom.

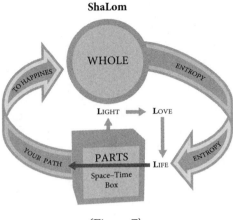

(Figure 7)

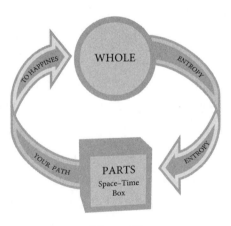

(Figure 8)

However, our work was not in vain. The ST box in which we exist is at a slightly higher level than it was before.

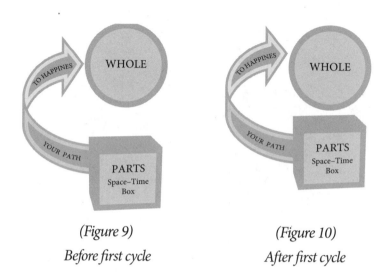

(Figure 9)
Before first cycle

(Figure 10)
After first cycle

We are familiar with this path. We can continue along our journey from this higher starting point. We are famliar with this path to happiness (Figure 11–17). We know that we must *Search for Light,* thinking on purpose. We must *Act with Love,* acting on purpose. We must then *Create a Life of Holiness* and *Seek ShaLom,* thinking and acting on purpose. Once again, we've raised the ST box and reached a moment of happiness. Inevitably, entropy returns, Light, Love, Life, and Shalom are disrupted, and so must we return once again to Y*our Path to Happiness.* We can navigate through this process of *Your Path to Happiness* using the four healing values with more ease each time this process is repeated. We also raise the ST box with each cycle.

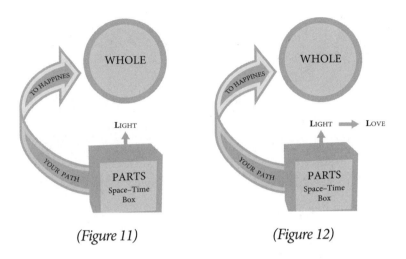

(Figure 11)   (Figure 12)

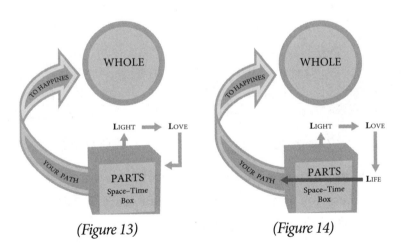

(Figure 13)   (Figure 14)

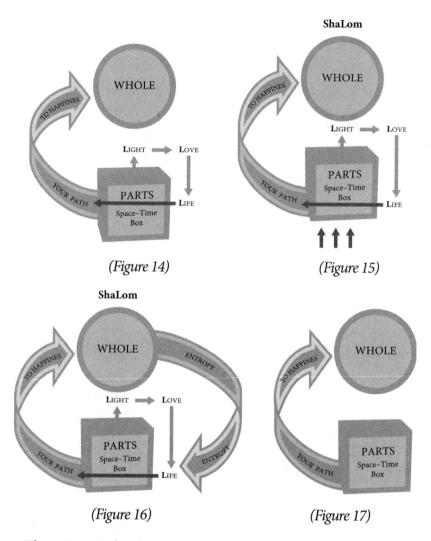

(Figure 14)

(Figure 15)

(Figure 16)

(Figure 17)

Thus, *Your Path to Happiness* is your story, your unique quest for success, joy and happiness. It is your journey using the four key healing values: Light, Love, Life, & ShaLom.

A question remains. The first time we leave the ST box, coming out of our universe of space and time, we partake in God's wholeness in the metaphysical realm. It is a parts-to-whole process that can fix the whole-to-parts creation of our

ST box. This seems to be the whole-parts-whole process we were looking for. This should be the end of the story! And yet we return to the parts and our lives inside the ST box. It is as if we had a ladder to God. God is in the metaphysical realm at the top of the ladder. If after climbing the ladder, we can once again experience ourselves in the presence of God, why in the world would we want to leave that presence and return to the parts by "going down the ladder?" If, as we saw in the first of the lessons of learning, we have real freedom of choice, *why in the world don't we stay in the metaphysical realm?* Why would we ever want to go back down the ladder? I say, "Kick that ladder away. Leave me alone. I want to stay here."

This leads us to the essence of thinking and acting on purpose. This is essential to both understanding our pain and our problems in life, and knowing how to heal from that pain and find solutions to those problems. What I propose is that **the reason we return is because it is our purpose**. We become God's messengers traveling down His ladder. We are God's angels; we are God's business partners, partners in the business of life. *We leave the comfort of the metaphysical summit to serve others on Earth.* We go back into the box. This is where the values from the lessons of learning are helpful. Remember, those values were freedom, responsibility, and purpose. We do have freedom, and we can use that freedom to choose to stay in the metaphysical realm, up on the summit with God's light shining warmly upon us. That is the focus of Eastern religion—Nirvana. Their focus is transcending this world. Judeo-Christian purpose is focused on transforming this world not on transcending it. Therefore, we do not stay forever at the metaphysical summit.

We can choose to use our *freedom* to stay on the summit or return to the ST box. We can act with *responsibility*. We can do the right thing. Responsibility is our response to our God-given abilities. In that higher realm, we are given an awareness of our special abilities to help and serve other people. Our higher *purpose* is to actualize those blessings. Part of our purpose, then, is to go back down into the ST box and actualize our higher purpose down in the natural world. Yes, we have freedom, but we need to remember that we also have responsibility to ourselves and others to do the right thing, to think and act on purpose. We cannot act in the metaphysical realm. We can only fix problems when we are inside the ST box. We must return to the natural world and actualize our purpose and fix the broken parts, as best as we can.

Interestingly, we are not completely free to choose to remain on the metaphysical summit. We can choose to come down willingly or unwillingly. Willingly is an act of love. Unwillingly has two possibilities. First of all, remember there is entropy. The tendency for disorder removed us from this highly ordered, meaningful, and purposeful realm.

Secondly, this "climb up the ladder" that we have made is a temporary situation. We have not completely left the ST box. We are still alive. We still have a physical aspect, our bodies. As long as we are alive, we cannot make a permanent connection outside the ST box. Even if we could make a deep connection outside the ST box, that is God's realm, and we lose some of our free will in that realm. He actually returns us to the ST box. As we return into the ST box, we have a choice of how to respond to that situation. Will we act as his messengers, accepting responsibility and acting as victors, or will we choose to act as victims, blaming and complaining?

For those two reasons, our temporary stay at the summit and the entropic ST box, we have no choice but to be returned to the pain and problems inside the ST box. The point is we can return begrudgingly or with responsibility. We can choose the ordinary response and act as a victim. We can be forced back down the ladder, complaining, "I don't want to do this; I don't want to do this!" Or we can choose the extraordinary response, to return with purpose. "So That___!" We can choose to take the tools and empowerment that we have gained in the metaphysical realm. We can return to earth, our ST box, bringing solutions and healing to ourselves and others with problems and pain.

Remember the story of my mother who recovered remarkably from open-heart surgery. She could have taken the role of the victim. The universe gave her a challenge. She would rather not have needed open-heart surgery. She could have blamed and complained. Not my mother! Instead, she turned it into a bigger challenge. From a state of wholeness and health, the entropic universe gave her a health problem with broken parts (a broken heart!). Searching for light, she climbed up to the metaphysical summit and made a timeless values connection. She reconnected with her key timeless value, her family. Her purpose became spending the upcoming Sabbath at home with her family, rather than mostly alone in a hospital. As an act of love to herself, she brought that purpose back with her into the ST box. Her goal was to heal from her Monday morning open-heart surgery in time to be discharged Friday afternoon and spend the Sabbath at home with her family. The power of that purpose empowered her to override the pain of her problems. We're talking about open-heart surgery pain. Now that's real pain! In the ST box, she used her purpose—her love of her family—to create a life of Holiness. By acting on purpose, she was able to direct her healing So That... she was home Friday evening. She spent the day in the holy space of her family in the holy time of the Sabbath. Her space-time box was now at a higher level. She had what we call Shabbat shalom: peace from the Sabbath day. She had joy and inner peace, i.e. happiness. She had peace from connecting to her purpose and acting upon that purpose. She actualized her potential in the ST box. That ST box was not only a space-time box; it was also a "So That___!" Box. It became a place where she could actualize her "So That___!"— her purpose. She raised her ST box, and in the process, she raised our ST box as well. Not only did we get to enjoy the Sabbath with her, but the lessons that we learned from her example changed our level of thinking and thus our ST box. She had achieved happiness at home. Was she happy during her recovery? We will discuss that question in the next chapter.

So, you see, we come back down from the metaphysical summit because we are God's messengers, God's angels. We come back down to the challenges, the parts inside our space-time box, to fix this broken world. Now, however, we have tools to fix the broken parts. We have made *The Timeless Values Connection*. As long as evil exists inside the box, that's where we belong, helping to eradicate that evil. As long as there is suffering and problems inside the box, that's where we belong, helping to heal the suffering and solve the problems. Until our universe inside the box is a place of total balanced harmonic unity, of shalom, that's where we belong. In other words, we must use our freedom to choose responsibility to come back and to act on purpose in our physical universe.

Light Love Life & Shalom
is
Your Path to Happiness at Work & at Home

Light	*the source of purpose*	Values
Love	*the purpose*	Virtues
Life	*where the purpose is actualized*	Vocation
ShaLom	*Happiness*	Victory

*Joy and inner peace coming
from actualizing purpose*

In summary, we leave the happy comfort of the whole when we are born. This is the **Whole to Parts Initial Universal Condition**. We try to get back to the whole, to happiness. That quest is *Your Path to Happiness. Your Path to Happiness* makes use of the four healing values to overcome challenges and achieve happiness. We must **Search for Light**: the source of enlightenment, understanding, and purpose. You must go out of the space-time box into the dimension from which the light comes, the metaphysical. There, we experience the **Timeless Values Connection** and focus on our *VALUES*. There, we learn that our purpose is to Love, to serve. The power of that purpose overrides the pain of our problems. We must **Act with Love**. We focus on love as a *VIRTUE*. A virtue is a value in action. We cannot fully serve others in the metaphysical dimension. So as an act of love, we return into our ST box. However, we are not the same parts that we were before. We bring back with us from the metaphysical realm healing values, especially the value of Love and Life. Life is where our purpose is actualized. We **Create a Life of Holiness**, a Life empowered by Love. We use God's holy values as a focus in our *VOCATION*, our productive daily life. In returning to the ST box, we showed that our purpose is not to transcend this world, but to transform this world. We **Seek Moments of ShaLom** by returning inside the ST box and performing acts of love, connection, and service. We create moments happiness and shalom inside the box. We can bring God, the Power & Loving Greater Than Ourselves, back into the ST box. We actually make the entire ST box, our universe, more whole.

We can focus on this *VICTORY*. However, since entropy is still operating and everyone the inside the box is not cooperating, the whole to parts initial Universal condition returns. The full cycle repeats itself over and over. However, after each cycle, the parts inside the ST box are more connected. The ST box is "higher," more whole, more filled with happiness and closer to the metaphysical arena. As Rabbi Tarfon said, "It is not up to us to finish the job, but neither are we free from the responsibility of doing some of the work." We can be happy doing the job, while working to achieve happiness at the end of the job.

Now it's time to move on to questions about happiness. What should be our expectations regarding happiness? What is happiness? How do we achieve happiness? Our next chapter will shine a little "Light" on the subject.

Path Principles

- We live in a world of parts, of paradox, of pluralism and of uncertainty, creating our pain and problems.

- Spirituality is the notion that there is more than simply a physical universe, a space-time box. **Spirituality is an awareness of a higher dimension.**

- Holiness is bringing that spirituality and metaphysical timeless values into your daily productive life.

- Whole-Parts-Whole / To be whole = SHALOM:

Solve problems
Heal pain
Address needs   AT WORK &   Your Path
Look to satisfy wants   AT HOME   →   to Happiness
Overcome challenges
Make opportunities

- _**Your Path to Happiness**_ is your journey from parts to whole, from problems to purpose, from pain to healing, from challenges to solutions, and from brokenness to shalom.

- _Your Path to Happiness_ consists of the following:

  Whole to Parts Initial Universal Condition: The Setup.

  Search for Light: Leaving the ST box and journeying into the spiritual realm.

Timeless Values Connection Thinking in the metaphysical realm (thinking on purpose).

Act with Love: Returning to the ST box to serve others (acting on purpose).

Create a Life of Holiness: Actualizing values (thinking & acting on purpose).

Seek Moments of ShaLom: Experiencing moments of wholeness, of happiness.

→ By **Thinking & Acting on Purpose** along the path through life, we take the ordinary and transform it into the extraordinary.

— CHAPTER 4: —
THINKING ABOUT HAPPINESS

Path Prescription #4: Setting Proper Expectations

Now let's focus on happiness. Our souls yearn for happiness. We believe that when we are successful we will be happy. Consider your answers to the following questions:

* Do you need to be successful to be happy?
* Are you successful now?
* Are you happy now?
* Do you need to have a life free of problems to be happy?
* Is there a difference between being happy and achieving happiness?
* What are your expectations?
* Do you expect happiness and success?
* Or do you expect problems, failure, and pain?

Failure or success, unhappy or happy, pain or glory—what is your story? Let's investigate these questions.

Happiness is one of the distinguishing features of the human being. While animals experience only pleasure and pain, for human beings there is meaning, value, and purpose as well. **Happiness is the joyful actualization of your meaning and purpose.** Happiness is thus the combination of both the physical and spiritual worlds. There is a material, physical, pleasure and pain aspect— **joy**. There is also a spiritual, values, meaning and purpose aspect— **inner peace**.

When thinking about happiness, I believe it is essential to separate the terms happy and happiness. Happy and happiness are two different words and therefore they represent two different ideas.

* **Happy is what you choose to _be_. Happiness is what you choose to _become_.**
* We are not only human beings. We are also human becomings.
* **Our mission is to be happy while becoming someone who achieves happiness.**
* Happy is a state of being, not a feeling.
* Happiness is a process of becoming – a practice that requires habit and ritual (path).
* Being happy is a choice we make at any moment (now).
* Happiness is choosing a future, it's a long-term process.
* Happy is a state achieved through **thinking** about your purpose.
* Happiness is achieved through **thinking and acting** on your purpose.
* Happy is something we realize, happiness is something we achieve.
* Happiness is an aspiration, a quest for joy and the

achievement of inner peace while on your path to a meaningful life.

* While striving to achieve happiness, we can be happy.
* Happiness is a full life well lived.

Brian Tracy states: "Happiness has been defined as the progressive realization of a worthy ideal. You can only be happy as long as you're working step by step toward something that is really important to you."[15] The power of your purpose overrides the pain of your problems, thus empowering you to be happy in any moment.

Dennis Prager points out that "Happiness is far more than a personal concern. It is also a moral obligation."[16] We do not enjoy being around others who are not happy. People also tend to act more ethically and morally when they're happy. Anyone can be unhappy, but true achievement involves struggling to be happy. Anyone can choose to be a victim or choose to be responsible. "Happiness is a battle to be waged, not a feeling to be awaited."[17]

Happy is often used to describe a feeling. However, here we are not talking about feelings. We are talking about a state of being. *Happy is a state of being that is the result of a decision that you make from the inside, regardless of conditions on the outside.* You have a purpose—a reason to be happy. Because you are thinking and acting on your purpose on your path to happiness, you can choose to be happy. A happy state of being is one in which you experience:

* Purposeful thinking that can lead to acting on your purpose.
* Hope—seeing a path to a positive future with honesty about present problems.
* Enjoying the journey, not just the destination.
* Gratitude.

Many people make inaccurate assumptions regarding the two words "happy" and "happiness". First, they assume that being happy is a feeling. Next, they assume that happiness is being happy. Happiness is thus a happy feeling that is the result of good things that happened to them. They seem to need an outside source for determining their inside happiness. Their belief is that they have very little control over how happy they are, because, after all, how can anyone control their feelings or what happens to them? It is only when they experience success that they feel happy. When they fail, they feel unhappy. Such people feel unhappy much of the time. Since life is so hard, has so many problems and so much pain, how can one ever be happy or have happiness? You may be one of these people. How can you become happier?

My favorite Albert Einstein quote can help us. (As a member of The National Speakers Association I feel that it is my duty to include at least one Albert Einstein quote in my book) Einstein said: "The significant problems we face today cannot be solved at the same level of thinking we were at when we created them."[18]

Isn't that remarkable? The significant problems we face today cannot be solved at the same level of thinking **we** were at when **we created them**! In other words, our biggest problems do not come from the problems themselves. Rather they are caused by the way we **think** about those problems. Our problems are not out there. They are in here—inside us. Our problems are caused by an interpretation that we make inside our brains about what's going on out there in the world. This is what we call a paradigm. It is a way of seeing the world. When Einstein says that solving problems requires better thinking, he means that we need better paradigms. This is especially true of our thinking about being happy or unhappy, happiness or unhappiness, success or failure, and our assumptions and expectations.

How then, do we achieve a new level of thinking? We do something that is called a paradigm shift. Let me share with you two of my own personal paradigm shift experiences. The first story will sharpen your understanding of how problems are created by and depend on your thinking. The second story addresses your thinking about success and failure.

It was a Monday morning in September 2009. My youngest daughter had just recently married and moved to Rochester, New York. I had just spent the weekend with her, and was on my way back to Chicago. Being a frequent flyer, I usually have my choice of seats and had my usual aisle seat. Because of my Parkinson's disease and frequent flyer status, I was able to get on board early. This enabled me to set up everything I needed for the flight, without bothering too many people in the process. After putting everything in its place, I sat down. I waited to put on my seatbelt until the passenger who would sit next to me arrived.

At this point I played the game of trying to determine who it is that will sit next to me. I always prefer someone who smiles, and someone who is friendly. Being a speaker, of course, I love to speak. This can be a real problem for someone who wants to be left alone. Actually, I usually ask some questions and let my seat mate do most of the talking, because I believe I can learn something from every individual I meet. I do not believe that these meetings are by accident. Well, little did I realize that I was about to learn a lot from the fellow who was to sit next to me.

He approached, and as soon as I saw him I realized that I had a problem. He was a strong man, probably in his early 30s. He was wearing a shirt and jeans, and had a jacket with him, nothing else. There was no question about his ethnic background. He not only looked to be a Middle Eastern Arab, but he was speaking Arabic on a cell phone. To say that he was not smiling would be a gross understatement. He looked completely haggard. Nervously, he looked at me and made his way into his seat, still on the cell phone speaking Arabic. He finished his phone call with the word Salem (goodbye). He began to stare out the window with a distinct frown. He had a look that was a combination of extreme nervousness with pent-up anger. This was not a happy camper. By the way, I was beginning to have a problem with my own "happiness level."

Now please understand, I speak in Israel every year or so. Israeli Arabs are often in my audience. I speak about valuing differences even beyond tolerating differences between people. I am the kind of person who tries not to prejudge others. But this was beyond any experience I had ever had before. This guy worried me. And if you ask my wife she will tell you I never worry about safety issues, especially when I should.

As we took off and the flight went along, he remained in a state of agitation that had me worried. I had no idea what I should do about this. So, in my typical fashion, I went into denial and decided to read. Now you would think that reading is about as neutral an activity as I could choose. However, let me tell you what book I had brought on board. It was a volume of the Talmud. For those unfamiliar with the Talmud, it is a 20 volume set of Jewish rabbinic stories and legal literature. It is second to the Bible in holiness to Jews. I learn one two-sided page per day and in 7 1/2 years complete the text. I brought it on board thinking I could catch up with the daily reading. I rarely gave any thought to who might be sitting next to me. Why would that matter? Well, now I'm a little worried. Do I take out and open the book with its English translation but clearly visible Hebrew text? Will he notice? Will he ask me about it? Or more importantly, upon seeing the text will he leap to his feet, whip out a weapon, take me hostage, slash my throat, and then detonate a hidden explosive device bringing down everyone aboard? Okay, maybe in retrospect this is a bit extreme, but it was a day in September, and this guy really looked nervous to the max.

I decided that cooler heads should prevail and I would just simply begin reading. He probably wouldn't even notice, being so self absorbed in some issue. I began reading and he noticed immediately. He was staring directly at the text, then at me, and then back to the text. He still looked very agitated, turned toward me, and said, "What book is this?"

Okay, I thought to myself, just go with the flow and you will probably avoid being tomorrow's headline. "This is a volume of the Talmud, a Jewish text from about the year 500," I said. "I read it every day for its teachings on Jewish law and life."

I finished the word life, hoping that this would not be the end of mine. He had no response. What do I do now? Well I did what I am paid to do, I continued speaking. I figured the best thing would be to just read from the Talmud to give him an idea of what it was like. Before I fully realized what I was reading, I had read to this guy a passage in the Talmud arguing for Jewish rights to the land of Israel. When the full impact of what I had read entered my conscious thought, I started shaking, and this was not Parkinson's shaking.

"Oh really," he said. "That is very interesting." Much to my relief he broke out into a huge smile! "My name is Ahmed. Please excuse me. I must seem unfriendly. It's just that I'm very concerned about my father. You see, I'm on my way back from Palestine where my father is in the hospital recovering from a heart attack. I am very concerned for his health and just got off the phone with him."

What followed was a fascinating conversation for the rest of the flight. It turns out that Ahmed was an American and Jordanian citizen. His family lived in Jordan and Palestine, and he visited there often. He owned several convenience stores here in the US. He hated the Hamas and was very critical of much of the Palestinian leadership. He spoke with deep emotion and concern for the future of his fellow Palestinians. I hope one day to send Ahmed this book.

That's what I mean by a paradigm shift.

A paradigm is our interpretation of our experiences. It is what we think happened to us. It is our understanding of what is really happening out there in the world. It is the eyeglasses through which we see the world. As you can see, our thinking can be very wrong. We do not see reality the way it is. Rather, we see reality the way we are. My initial assumptions about Ahmed were not correct. As soon as I saw him, I saw the potential for him to be a terrorist. Once I assumed that he was a terrorist, every interpretation of what I saw was based on that initial assumption. All the problems, worries, and fears that ensued were caused by that thinking.

However, my initial assumption was wrong. He was not a terrorist at all, quite the contrary. He was a loving son filled with concern about his father's life threatening situation and his future health. Upon hearing the information about his father, a light went on in my head. I became enlightened about my false assumptions and began switching the interpretations, one after another, until I had a completely revised view of the situation. From then on I enjoyed the rest of the flight and learned quite a bit from Ahmed.

This switching of interpretations is what we call a paradigm shift. It is a shift in thinking that is extremely powerful and it can help solve most of our problems. As Einstein noted, our problems come from our thinking. Thus the easiest way to solve our problems is through better thinking. Why is that? Our thoughts and our values become our words, our words become our actions, our actions become our habits, our habits become our character, and our character becomes our destiny. We become what we think about. We become what we value. If we want to solve our problems, we need to have the right values, the right thinking, and the right actions. It all starts with better thinking.

Using better thinking you will find yourself questioning your assumptions in almost any situation that arises. It is then that you should ask yourself these questions— What if I am wrong? And then what? Revisit your initial assumptions along the way using new information to test the truth of your old assumptions. If necessary, shift your paradigm. If not, keep testing it as time goes on. This will be discussed in greater detail in the next chapter.

I want to point out here that terrorists do exist. We need to be aware of this reality. We cannot "think" it away. Ahmed was not a terrorist. My paradigm shift message was not that since I thought Ahmed was a terrorist and he turned out not to be a terrorist, that anyone looking or acting like Ahmed is also not a terrorist. That would be a mistake. We must keep all of our paradigm options open. We must continually test them against reality.

The message for you here is to test your assumptions about being happy, having happiness, and understanding success and failure and its role in happiness. Your paradigms need testing. The following story addresses these issues.

I must take you back to my Little League days in the 1960s. The star of the team was always the pitcher. Everybody wanted to be the pitcher. Although I really enjoyed playing shortstop (I loved to watch the White Sox infielders Luis Apparicio and Nellie Fox play), people kept pushing me to try out for pitcher. After a while I thought that they must be right. How could I be happy if I wasn't successful, and people kept telling me that success in Little League was being a successful pitcher?

My coach let me pitch at the start of an exhibition game. The first batter came up to the plate and I was nervous as can be. But I wound up, let the ball go, and threw a perfect strike. I followed that with two more and struck out the first batter. I thought, "I'm good, I'm good."

The next batter up was a lefty and he gave me a look that said, "I'm taking you downtown." I gave him a look back that said, "I have no idea what your look is saying." In any case three pitches and he was gone! Strikeout number two! At this point I was thinking of a big Major League contract.

The third batter up was a big kid. I never looked directly at him. I was too scared to even see the kind of look he might be giving me. I felt a lot of air from his swing, but the ball never touched his bat. Three strikes and we are out of the inning. At this point I was thinking Hall of Fame—no question.

It was so cool to come to the bench. Clearly a new star had been born. This must be what happiness is all about. Happiness comes from being successful.

Unfortunately, there was a second inning. It did not start anywhere near as well as the first. I walked the first batter on four pitches. Then I walked the second batter on four pitches. This was followed by the third batter loading the bases. And then I walked the fourth, fifth, and sixth batters, giving up three runs without a ball out of the infield—or without a ball even in the infield for that matter. The coach shouted from the bench for me to let him hit it. Well…after the grand slam and seven runs, I found myself back at shortstop. I failed as a pitcher. I had lost. At the time I was truly embarrassed, and I felt the pain of loss. I was definitely not a happy camper.

Had I really failed? I tried hard, wasn't that enough? Life is not about trying—it is about getting results. If you have a good surgeon and he tries his best and you die—you don't care! I clearly had a bad outcome. I lost in the short run. But in the long run, I got to play shortstop, which I loved and, as it turned out, was a position in which I played well.

Was I a failure, was I a loser? To paraphrase Robert Kiyosaki,[19] **in life we either win or learn.** As I like to add, **if we learn we almost never lose.**

I learned that I was not a very good pitcher. I learned I was much better at shortstop.
<u>SO THAT</u> I could become a better shortstop,
I needed to learn the lesson that I was <u>NOT</u> a pitcher.

As it turned out, I had an all-star year as shortstop! Our team won the title with a pitcher who was much better than I was. But at shortstop, I was the best. **The only problem I**

had was my thinking about the problem—my paradigm.
I was thinking that the only way to be my best at Little
League required me to be a pitcher. That was bad thinking,
a bad paradigm based on bad assumptions. Not only did I
assume I needed to be a pitcher, but I assumed that I could
have success without any suffering, without any difficulty.
I experienced pain, suffering, and unhappiness from my
unmet expectations, thinking I was a failure. Ultimately
I did not fail. I won because I learned. I adjusted my
thinking. I adjusted my expectations; therefore, I shifted
my paradigm.

Often our expectations do not match up with reality. Unmet
expectations cause stress and suffering. Losing causes
suffering. When we suffer, most of us are not happy. At this
point we have a choice. As we have discussed in the lessons of
learning, we can act responsibly (win-learn) or we can blame
(win-lose). When we suffer, it is far easier to blame than to
take responsibility and solve our problems. We want to play
the victim and blame someone or something. Why not go to
the top and blame the big guy? Blame God.

We see it all the time, don't we? "God, why did you let my
mother die of cancer? God why do you let there be wars in
this world?" We blame God for the big problems that we
face. As lots of folks in Chicago ask, "God, why can't you let
the Cubs win the World Series? Blaming God would be the
ordinary response to your problems.

Instead of blaming God, shift your paradigm. Imagine choosing an extraordinary response to your problems. This involves acting *responsibly, thinking, and acting on purpose,* using the power of purpose to overcome even the pain of problems and choose to be happy. Then, imagine having *gratitude* to God for those problems.

Gratitude? Come on Steinberg. Are you kidding me? How can we be grateful to a God who allows us to suffer from problems?

"Hey God...thanks for the Parkinson's disease. I really appreciate getting this disorder that won't allow me to make a living doing what I love while helping people. Thank you sooo much!!!!!!!"

That is precisely the challenge of God's expectations from us. M. Scott Peck in his classic book *The Road Less Traveled* states, "Life is difficult... life is a series of problems. Do we want to moan about them or solve them?"[20] Peck is saying that the **ordinary** response is to moan and groan about life's problems.

Life expects more from you. Life asks you to shift your paradigm. Life asks you to respond extraordinarily, to accept responsibility and focus on solving your problems by thinking and acting on purpose. Those problems are messengers with a message for you to change your thinking or change your actions. Solutions to those problems are also sent to you by God as messages from his messengers. The most powerful message is *"Change your thinking about your problems."* That means changing your *expectations*—expect short-term problems; accept responsibility—look for solutions; *think and act on purpose*—on Your Path to Happiness; *and be happy* along the path.

Anthony Robbins[21] points out that pain is a signal for you to change. There are only two things that you can change—your beliefs or your behavior. As I like to put it, you can only change your thinking or your actions. Pain is thus your messenger with a message to change your thinking or your acting.

Brian Tracy puts it this way, "Whenever God gives us a gift he wraps it up in a problem. The bigger the gift, the bigger the problem."[22]

Like God Himself, his messengers as well as his messages are often hidden. They do not show up with a sign on their chest—I am a messenger. Remember God has withdrawn. He is hidden. Even so, we can find him. Even though happiness is hidden, we can find it. That was certainly true for me as a pitcher. All I knew was that I had failed and that hurt. Hidden from me at the time was the fact that the pain of failure can be a message to learn and to change.

<u>SO THAT</u> I could become a better shortstop, I needed to learn the lesson that I was <u>NOT</u> a pitcher.

It was my responsibility to win or learn. *Looking to learn I can also win.* Some messengers help you win and some help you learn. I needed to learn the lesson of accepting responsibility, and often so do you. That is why messengers are sent to you, and they sometimes come in the form of a significant loss. You need to be looking to learn so that you can also win.

It is *your responsibility* to **find** your hidden messengers.
It is *your job* to **understand** their messages (Light).
It is then *up to you* to **act** accordingly (Love).
Finally, it is *up to you* to have **gratitude and be happy** for the messenger and the message (Life-Shalom).

Armed with this powerful paradigm of win/learn, *of learning how to change our thinking about problems to help solve our problems,* let us see if this will help further our understanding of happiness.

Remember two of the assumptions people make about success and happiness that we discussed earlier. First of all, people assume that happiness depends on being successful. Anytime we have success, we feel happy; but when we fail, we feel unhappy. The solution to this first assumption is to use better thinking to define success as either winning or learning. Either way we are successful. When we learn we can be happy, even though in theory we lost. I thought I'd lost, failed, because I was a lousy pitcher and had no other alternative path to be successful. In that condition, I could not have happiness because there was no path for success. According to this assumption, the only way I could have happiness was to experience success. However, upon rethinking my situation, I realized I could be a successful shortstop. By changing my thinking in regards to what defines *success,* I could still have success and therefore happiness.

That leaves us with the assumption that we seem to need some outside source in order to be happy inside. Okay, I did not have to be a successful pitcher to be happy, but I did need to be at least a successful shortstop to be happy. At a first level of thinking, I changed my definition of success. Here comes the real trick. Second level thinking about being happy requires a process that empowers us to be happy even when we're not successful. Can we possibly be happy when things aren't going well? Could I be happy if I failed at being a shortstop too? How could I control my feelings if I was constantly challenged by failure? How can any amount of thinking overcome feelings?

I don't want you to simply *read* my answer; I want you to *experience* my answer. To accomplish this I will bring you two experiences.

First, here is another story about my mother, I think you're beginning to see that she is my happiness hero. She has been an incredible role model for me when it comes to happiness. Several years ago she was on a cruise in the Caribbean. One of the stopovers was on an island where there was snorkeling and other activities. She went snorkeling in the morning and scraped her legs twice on some coral rocks. Not only was she sore from the scrape itself, but she had a severe inflammatory reaction from the coral.

As we already know, a little pain is not going to stop my mother from doing something she wanted to do. So, even with some significant pain, she went diving later that day. This was the first and only time she ever went diving. Her first time down a weight belt fell off requiring her to surface. When she went back down the second time, she didn't clear her ears properly, and so she suffered a bruised eardrum from the water pressure. The net result of the day was a very inflamed and painfull bruise and scrape to her legs along with a painfully bruised eardrum.

As my mom tells the story, those were just things that happened to her on that wonderful day. Why was that day wonderful? It was because of purpose. Not only does the power of purpose override the pain of problems, but notice, she was *happy* doing these things that caused her *pain*! She did more than override the pain; she ignored it to the point where she was happy. How did she do that? Once again the answer is purpose. My mother happens to be a retired University biology professor. (Part of her purpose in life is to learn about and see every single living thing in the universe. (My mother does not set low goals.)

When she told me the story, she said she would do it all again in an instant. I asked her, "Why? You were in pain." She explained that under the water she was able to go up and down, back and forth, along a 35 foot floating wall teaming with life. It was exotic, varied, and beautiful. It was an underwater zoo. She saw things that she had never seen before. As a PhD in invertebrate zoology, she had seen a lot before. But on this coral, for the first time, she saw Christmas tree worms, crabs everywhere, anemones, shrimp, and coral. Floating around it was an amazing array of saltwater fish. It was just beautiful.

The diving coach who went down with my mother later said, "I thought we would have to pull this lady up by her heels, she didn't want to stop. Not only that, she used very little oxygen. Usually, people come up after their first dive gasping for breath. She was down there just staring and pointing, fascinated by everything she was looking at, using hardly any oxygen." Whenever we asked my mother to tell the story again, she finished the story saying, "I would do it again in an instant."

Her motivation was internal not external. External motivation comes to us when we feel that we don't have enough of something that we like to get. This is because as human beings we are never fully satisfied. We never get *enough, and never feel completely successful. And since* success is the external factor by which we judge the situation, we are never happy. Internal motivation comes to us from the desire to engage in an activity because we value it for the inherent satisfaction that it provides us. You would do it for free. Your motivation comes from inside of you. You do not need anything else to supply motivation for you to be happy. You are happy because you are doing exactly what you were put on this earth to do. That is your "reason for being happy." That makes you happy from the inside out. In fact, because the power of purpose overrides the pain of problems, your motivation to do what you're doing can be so strong, as in the case of my mother, that you ignore real pain.

My mother always chooses to be happy in any moment while striving for achievement of her goals and purposes over the long term. Here we begin the transition from a focus of being happy to a focus of achieving happiness. **Happy is what we choose to be; happiness is what we choose to become.** My mother chose to be happy in that short term moment, while striving for happiness in the long term.

As we said earlier, Brian Tracy states: "Happiness has been defined as the progressive realization of a worthy ideal." The power of your purpose overrides the pain of your problems, thus empowering you to be happy in any moment. That same power of purpose can empower you to actualize and achieve that purpose itself. Seeing and experiencing the underwater wall brimming with life was one step in my mother's progressive realization of her goal to experience the abundance of life forms on the planet Earth.

Happiness is experiencing joy and inner peace.

Tal Ben-Shahar, in his book *Happier*, defines happiness as, "the overall experience of pleasure and meaning." He goes on to say, " A happy person enjoys positive emotions while perceiving her life as purposeful. The definition does not pertain to a single moment but to a generalized aggregate of one's experiences: a person can endure emotional pain at times and still be happy overall."[23] My mother has hardly lived a pain free life. She spent much of her childhood with rheumatic fever and she lost her four-year-old daughter, my sister, to Tay-Sachs disease. While focusing on purpose and meaning, on her remaining children, she was able to be happy overall during the whole experience of life rather than focusing on the pain of any one negative experience.

While striving to achieve happiness we can be happy.

Tal Ben Shahar notes, "Attaining lasting happiness requires that we enjoy the *journey* on our way toward a *destination* we deem valuable. Happiness is not about making it to the peak of the mountain nor is about climbing aimlessly around the mountain; *happiness is the experience of climbing toward the peak*."[24] My mother is always having a peak experience during her climb!

Happiness is a practice that requires habit and ritual. Marci Shimoff, in her book *Happy for No Reason*, quotes Stewart Emery, "In 1776 to pursue something meant to practice that activity, to do it regularly, to make a habit of it." Therefore what Jefferson meant was that "we all have the right to **practice happiness**, not chase after it. So let's stop pursuing happiness and start practicing it. We do that by practicing new habits."[25] Professionals practice their profession. We will learn more about that in Chapter 9. We must practice our human profession: our path to happiness.

Shimoff states, "What we are all really looking for is happiness from within that doesn't depend on external circumstances—the kind I call *Happy for No Reason*... No matter what my external circumstances are, there is still a feeling of unshakable fulfillment, joy, and inner peace."[26] She goes on to say, "It's a state that's been spoken of in virtually all spiritual and religious traditions throughout history. The concept is universal. In Buddhism, it is called causeless joy, in Christianity, the Kingdom of Heaven within, and in Judaism it is called *Ashrei*, an inner sense of holiness and health. In Islam it is called *falah*, happiness and well-being, and in Hinduism it is called *ananda*, or pure bliss. Some traditions refer to it as an enlightened or awakened state."[27]

When I read Shimoff speaking of happy for no reason, I always hear myself thinking happy for no *external* reason.

Viktor Frankl pointed out "happiness cannot be pursued; it must ensue. One must have a reason to 'be happy.' Once the reason is found, however, one becomes happy automatically." [28] I believe that Shimoff, Viktor Frankl, and I are actually in agreement with the concepts, but are using different words to describe the concepts. **Happy is a state of being, happiness is a process of becoming—a practice.** Being happy is a choice we make at any moment. It requires better thinking. Happiness is a long term process of thinking *and acting* on purpose. It is a search for joy and inner peace. Happiness emerges from the process of the practice of living life.

Since happiness requires acting as well as thinking, it requires some level of achievement, of accomplishment. Results are necessary. We can choose our particular quest for happiness; we cannot choose the outcome, the results. We are not in complete control. Outside factors are involved. Tornadoes, hurricanes, earthquakes, and tsunamis get in the way. However, we can always choose our response to those outcomes. While on the path to happiness we can choose to be happy at any moment. We also can choose to win or learn regardless of our outside conditions, our present results.

Happiness can be based solely on external circumstances or in combination with your internal character. You can choose to be a victim of external circumstances or a victor using your internal character and choosing an extraordinary response. I chose to be a victim while trying out for pitcher.

In the first inning my external circumstances were that I was winning. Since I was winning I was happy. However, in the second inning my external circumstances were that I was losing horribly. Since I was losing horribly I was terribly unhappy. That's being a victim. As Einstein said, I chose my problem, I myself created my own problem by the way I saw my problem and by my thinking.

Now what's important here is that I really did lose. But the instant after I lost I had a choice to make. The choice was not did I "actually" win or lose. By the rules of the game I was playing I lost. However, I was playing two games. The first game was a game of baseball and I lost. As soon as that game finished, the second game began. The second game was the game of life. My rule in the game of life is that if I lose, then as soon as is possible, I try to learn from the experience. I look for messengers with a message. As soon as I learn, I win in the game of life. Immediately after potential victimhood, I respond to my conditions with responsibility by learning from the experience. This is Einstein thinking. This thinking is internal—it's going on in my head. In choosing responsibility, I choose to be happy for internally good reasons. I am happy because of my internal thinking. I am happy for no reason, for no *external* reason.

The lesson of being happy for no external reason is one I learned from my mother's experiences. I wanted you to "experience" her story, to learn the lesson that she has taught me. Now I want to relate a second experience related to inside versus outside thinking. I want to relate an experience about overcoming emotional challenges using better thinking and better paradigms. It is my experience each day with Parkinson's disease. Let me tell you about parts of my typical day.

I get up at 4:00 AM. For years I have been an early riser. However I get up even earlier than I used to because of how long it takes me to do things with Parkinson's disease. When I wake up, most of the benefits of my medications have worn out. I wake up stiff, with some locking of my limbs, making it hard to get out of bed.

When I get out of bed, I do the Parkinson's shuffle off to the bathroom (No relationship to the 1985 Super Bowl shuffle—sorry Bears fans). It is always interesting to wash my hands and face first thing in the morning. I turn on the water, put a bar of soap in one hand, and try to "quickly" rub the other hand back and forth over the soap. Watching me, you would think you were watching a replay in super slow motion. I now use liquid soap, which is better, but still difficult. I find it interesting, both as a medical professional watching my disease from the inside out, and as a curiosity to see how well I will do each day. Since I do not have medications on board, I do not shave or finish in the bathroom, nor do I get dressed. Once the medicines are working I can do all those things quicker.

Next, I go downstairs to get my medicines. I have realized that I made a big mistake in not buying stock in medicine companies. Each morning I take four Parkinson's medications, nine mineral vitamin pills, ground flax seed (the medications cause constipation), and a white powdery substance in an unmarked white packet. The unmarked packet is from a study in which I am participating and it contains an experimental drug (I hope) or a placebo (my luck?).

Interestingly, as an international speaker, I was once in Chile. I was going through my morning ritual of medication when I started getting a little bit nervous. Nothing happened on the way down, but I started wondering what would happen on the way back if customs officials got a look at my packets. Let's see, unmarked white packets with a "white powder" inside?? Now that could look a bit suspicious. I can hear the officials now, "An experimental medicine?! What kind of fools do you take us for—take him away." On my way back home, I had finished virtually all of the packets so it wasn't a big deal. I reported this to my doctor who said, "I'll give you a note for the next time you travel." Wow! What a big help that will be—a note! I'm sure they will believe that.

In any case, at this point in time I have some breakfast and then start my fun by trying to get dressed. I have always been slow at doing things, I do have the nickname "turtle-toes," but sometimes it takes me so long to get dressed I end up in another time zone. My greatest challenge is buttoning my shirt. For many shirts I pre-button them and put them on as if there are no buttons. The second task is putting on my pants. For that I figured out a trick. Because it was taking me a long time to close the front of my pants, they would start falling down before I could get them closed (okay, please do not laugh too hard as you picture that in your mind). The trick is to pull up the pants and lean back against a wall so that the pants don't fall. This gives me more time to close everything in front. Once I am dressed, down I go into my home office and begin to work. Usually this is around 5:30 AM.

When I am writing my books or speeches I must use a voice-activated system, because I cannot type very well at all. Of course I never could type very well, but at least now I have a big excuse. I like the system but it doesn't always work (go figure, technology that doesn't work perfectly, who would've thought?). With my shaking, using a mouse is of course a big challenge, but I try to do my best.

The next challenge is remembering to take my pills on time. If I do forget, my tensing jaw, weird facial expression, and general shaking eventually reminds me. In addition to the four Parkinson's pills in the morning, I take two pills three more times each day. That's a total of ten Parkinson's pills each day. I take nine more of the mineral vitamins at night and one additional white packet at night. So in total I do two packets and 28 pills each day. Retail, I do $12,000 of medications per year. I will say this, "Anyone who complains about drug companies can come and talk to me." The quality of my life would be massively worse without those medications. It required years of research for some of these medications to be formulated. The benefits that I get are priceless. May they live long and prosper, and find better drugs each year.

Often, in the evening, the medications wear out before I get to bed. So I shuffle off to bed. I go to sleep, and you might think that's the end of that, but wait. It turns out that I dream loudly, shouting commands and shrieking in horror as I try to save the galaxy from aliens. My wife has figured out a series of karate moves to wake me up so that I will stop having that particular dream and let her go back to sleep. She has actually been wonderful about this whole disorder. In any case, before I know it it's 4:00 AM and up I go again.

"Why me?"

It all seems to come back to that question. However, we have moved well beyond that initial question along our path to happiness. We have discovered that in life you either win or you learn. You can change a loss into a win if you learn from the loss. Pain and problems can be a great messenger for you to change your thinking and/or your actions. That's what I've learned from my Parkinson's disease. It is my messenger with many messages.

Make no mistake about it: getting Parkinson's disease is a loss. It is a big loss. In and of it itself it does not make me happy.

In fact in and of itself it makes me unhappy. The question is how do I respond to having Parkinson's disease? Do I have the character to come back from this loss and win? Can I choose to learn? Can I change my thinking? Can I change my paradigm? Can I change my acting? Ultimately it's my choice. I am responsible. That is what we've learned so far.

As Rob Stearns says in his book *Winning Smart after Losing Big,* **"You lose because you are human. You win because you are *you.*"[29]**

As a human being you are guaranteed that at some point in your life you will lose. However, as an individual, because of your unique inner character, because you are you, you have within yourself the ability to turn any loss into a win.

As a human being, at times I will fail. As a human being, at times I will make mistakes. As a human being I will suffer from problems, challenges, and pain. As a human being, I will lose, often. All of that is guaranteed. What is not guaranteed is how I respond to losing. It *is* hard for me to get dressed in the morning, it *is* hard for me to work on the computer and it *is* hard to have Parkinson's disease. Even with the Parkinson's disease, however, I have choice. I choose to be a happy person. I choose to focus on the good that I'm experiencing at each moment and not the bad. They are both present.

There are things that are hard for me to do on a daily basis because of Parkinson's disease. However that does not mean

I'm generally unhappy. Even with the Parkinson's disease I am a happy person. I'm happy because I think of those problems as external things and I have no control over them. I take a long term view hoping that I will be better in the future. In the short term I can be happy because I am on purpose. I have my "reason for being happy." I love speaking and writing. I'm able to "leap out of bed" happy to face another day because I know I will get to do things that I love doing.

The power of my purpose overrides the pain of my Parkinson's problems. I believe that things will work out in the long term. Will it be difficult in the short term? Of course. However, I'm not wasting my time moaning about how this is a non-curable disease and I'm not complaining about the degeneration that will probably take place over time. In fact, I often make fun of this whole experience as you may have noticed. I laugh at myself and I joke about it. That laughter is quite therapeutic and healing.

Is this life difficult? Yes, of course it's hard. In the movie *A League of Their Own*, Tom Hanks plays the manager of a women's baseball team. He finds his star player getting ready to quit and leave the team. He says to her, "Sneaking out like this, quitting, you'll regret it for the rest of your life. Baseball is what gets inside you. It's what lights you up, you can't deny that." She replies to him, "It just got too hard." He responds to her with one of the best lines I've ever heard in a movie: "It's supposed to be hard. If it wasn't hard, everyone would do it. The hard...is what makes it great."

It is not easy to do the right thing for a lifetime. The challenge is day-to-day. We all have tough issues to be faced. That's the point. Life is difficult. We cannot cure this condition. However, we can heal. The focus needs to be on healing over time—of striving for happiness. We need to travel along our path to long term joy and inner peace. Happiness is a lifetime quest that requires overcoming challenges and problems. Whether we meet those challenges in the long term or not, in the short term we can be happy. We can approach each day with gratitude for our blessings and for the messengers with their messages and lessons.

Here are the steps for success after any loss:

1. Feel the pain of the loss.

    That feeling, that pain, is a signal to change. It is your message to yourself: "Houston we have a problem!" Feelings are a messenger with a message to change your thinking or acting.

2. Shift from feeling to thinking as soon as possible.

    Feelings do not solve problems. As Einstein pointed out, our problems are related to our thinking. Therefore switch from feeling to thinking as soon as possible.

3. Identify the cause of the loss. Was it due to:

    a. Poor thinking (a bad plan or poor expectations)? In that case, change your thinking.

    b. Inappropriate acting (poor implementation of the plan)? Here you must change your behavior or acting.

    c. Just bad luck (fire, hurricanes etc.)? Here you must stay on track.

4. Propose solutions using the four healing values: Use Light, Love, Life, and ShaLom to connect back to thinking and acting on your purpose.

5. Choose one solution.

6. Create a plan of action.

7. Act.

8. Review.

You win after losing because you are you. You are a unique and special individual who was put on this Earth to win in some unique and special way—your way. I win because I am me. I was put here for some unique and special purpose. Using my character, I can choose to win or learn. As Peter Senge says in his book *The Fifth Discipline*, "Real learning gets to the heart of what it means to be human. Through learning we re-create ourselves. Through learning we become able to do something we never were able to do. Through learning we extend our capacity to create, to be part of the generative process of life. There is within each of us a deep hunger for this type of learning."[30]

Now every day, all day long, in response to my conditions and circumstances, such as my Parkinson's disease, I have a series of choices to make. My choices are based on my paradigm—my thinking about life. I can choose between victim thinking, happy thinking, and happiness thinking. You have that same choice every day.

The differences between victim thinking, happy thinking, and happiness thinking are based on whether the focus is internal or external in *space* (inside or outside my mind) or past, present, or future in *time*. As a victim, your focus is external in space and in the past in time. You focus on blaming, complaining, and explaining away things to others. You never take responsibility, for issues lie outside of you. As a victim your focus in time is always the past. Rehashing, revisiting, moaning, and groaning about the past is your pastime. Without any future focus, how can you solve your problems? Victim thinking is very dangerous. It increases your pain and problems, and offers no solutions that will work in the long run. As a victim you never can have gratitude and therefore can never be happy. I never want to be a victim.

Instead of thinking as a victim you can choose to be a victor and be happy. As a happy person your focus is internal in space while your focus in time is the present—now. A happy person has a reason to be happy. But that reason is focused internally, based on your values, meaning, and your purpose. Because it is focused internally, external conditions are essentially irrelevant. Inside yourself you make the decision whether you will be happy at any instant. Happy now is an enduring, deeply based sense of peace of mind, knowing that everything is ultimately for the good. It requires connecting to the Power and Loving Greater Than Ourselves and paying attention to his messengers and their message to think and act on purpose. To paraphrase Joel Osteen, happy is a decision you make, rather than an emotion that you feel.[31] This might come as a surprise to most of us who believe that happy is a feeling. You need to make the feelings that you have be a consequence of your thinking and acting on purpose. Most people have it the other way around, experiencing conditions and basing all their actions on their feelings of the experience. This leads to victimhood. You become a victim of your feelings.

Happy people are happy now. The key to better thinking in the present is to have hope for the future. As previously mentioned, hope is seeing a path to a better future with honesty about present problems. Hope is seeing God's messengers all around you, ready to help you if and when you need help. Believing in this blessing one can only be happy in the moment.

What, then, is the focus of happiness? Is happiness found on the inside or outside? Is happiness found in the past, present or future? The answer is yes! The solution to this paradox is to realize that **happiness is the whole that emerges from a life well lived, a life lived on purpose, and a life with a purpose based on timeless values.** Happiness, being the whole, takes all these different parts and harmonizes them. The location of our focus must be internal *and* external. Our focus in time must be past, present, *and* future. Balancing, harmonizing, and unifying our life requires a dual ST focus: a focus in **Space** and **Time**, and a focus on your purpose, your "So That___!"

Happiness is experiencing both joy and inner peace. The joy can be from pleasure or the joy can be from meaning. Inner peace is the balanced harmonization and unification of all the different parts in your life working together as a whole. That process, the struggle leading to inner peace, is *Your Path to Happiness*. Emerging from that balanced harmonious unity is shalom. Shalom here is the concept of inner peace—it is the same thing as happiness. Happiness is an emergent property. It ensues and emerges from being happy (being joyful) and from doing things that are worthwhile to you. Happiness emerges from thinking and acting on purpose. On purpose living is *Your Path to Happiness*. Happiness ensues when we accept responsibility and actualize our potential.

Happiness is not achieved equally by every person. It requires knowledge and thinking, action and behavior, and practice. One needs an actualization protocol for happiness. One also needs good fortune and conditions in life conducive to achieving happiness. If one is in the wrong place at the wrong time, a deadly earthquake can end your quest for happiness. Happiness is an aspiration, a quest. You are never finished with that journey. While you are alive you are always on a path—always becoming.

We never experience complete happiness in this world. We are not just human beings, being happy. We are also human becomings, journeying along the path to becoming people who achieve happiness.

Now we can ask the question, "Should we raise our expectations or lower them?" The answer is "Yes." This I call the expectations paradox. Unmet expectations can be a tremendous source of pain and problems. So one answer would be to lower your expectations or have none at all.

What about hope, faith, belief, positive attitudes, positive thinking, and positive self talk? Those lead to the concept that we should have high expectations. So, should we raise our expectations or lower them? Once again the answer is "Yes." Expectations must be put into a context. In the short run, we should lower our expectations. We can expect pain and problems. That's why we're on this Earth—to solve each other's problems. We need to have problems so that we can achieve our purpose by solving them. In the long run, we need to have faith that we will be successful. We need to have faith that it will be worth our while to make the attempt to do something extraordinary. We must have faith that God would not have put us here to solve problems that we could not ultimately solve. So we raise our expectations. We know that along the way we will have pain—a messenger—signaling us with a message that we must change our thinking or our acting. At that point we must learn. I must understand how I really lose in the short run so that I can understand how to really win in the long run. It's important not to change the rules, the definitions of win and lose, in the middle of the game. In this game of life, I can take a short term loss and, by learning from it, I can turn it into a long term win. We must focus on the long term success that we envision. But we must start out with at least a basic concept that what we are doing is achievable thus having positive expectations about that possibility.

The truth is that Happiness is largely, although not entirely, determined by us from the inside out. By hard work, controlling our nature, and gaining wisdom we can achieve happiness. As Dennis Prager states, "Everything worthwhile in life requires work and happiness is no exception."[32]

Thinking, learning, and acting on that learning is hard, but it is the secret to long term success and happiness. In life we can win or learn. Basing your behavior and your actions on that learning empowers you to actualize your potential and achieve extraordinary results, leading to achieving happiness. But how do we know that our thinking is accurate? How do we know the truth? That's the next chapter —how do you know?

Path Principles

- Happy is what you choose to _be_; happiness is what you choose to _become_.

- Our mission is to be happy while becoming someone who achieves happiness.

- Happiness is the joyful actualization of your meaning and purpose.

- Happy is a state of being that is the result of a decision that you make from the inside, regardless of conditions on the outside.

- Einstein said: "The significant problems we face today cannot be solved at the same level of thinking we were at when we created them."

- A paradigm is our interpretation of our experiences.

- To paraphrase Robert Kiyosaki: In life we either Win or Learn. As I like to add, if we learn we almost never lose.

- Happy is a state of being, happiness is a process of becoming—a practice.

- Being happy is a choice we make at any moment. It requires better thinking.

- Happiness is a long term process of thinking _and acting_ on purpose.

- As Rob Stearns says, "You lose because you are human. You win because you are _you_."

* Life is difficult. We cannot cure this condition. However, we can heal.

* The focus needs to be on healing over time while at the same time striving for happiness.

* Happiness is a lifetime quest that requires overcoming challenges.

* Happiness is the whole that emerges from a life well lived.

* Whether we meet our challenges in the long term or not, in the short run we can be happy.

* We can approach each day with gratitude for our blessings and for the messengers with their messages and lessons.

Here are the steps for success after any loss:

1. Feel the pain of the loss.
2. Shift from feeling to thinking as soon as possible.
3. Identify the cause of the loss. Was it due to thinking, acting, or luck?
4. Propose solutions using the four healing values and choose one solution.
5. Create a plan of action.
6. Act.
7. Review.

— CHAPTER 5: —
HOW DO YOU KNOW?

Path Prescription #5: Knowing 101—The Ladder of Learning

As we learned in the last chapter, happy is what you choose to be while happiness is what you choose to become. Being happy is a choice we make at any moment. It requires better thinking. Happiness, on the other hand, is a long term process of thinking **and** acting on purpose. How do you know if your thinking is correct? How do you know if you are acting on purpose? How do you know your purpose? How do you know anything?

"How do you know?" is my father's favorite question, and one that I learned from him. Regardless of the topic or subject that we are discussing, whatever statement or claim that I make he responds with, "How do you know?" He is really asking, "How can you connect to the truth? What system of thinking can you use to become enlightened, and to turn that understanding into practical activities that lead to happiness?"

Our conversations cover science and religion, ethics and politics, and quite often dentistry. You see, my father is also a dentist. Actually, my father *is* a dentist, and I am *also* a dentist. I have followed in *his* footsteps. You can imagine how exciting it was for my children to listen to conversations around the dinner table whenever my father came over, as we would often focus on dentistry. When we spoke, I knew that any claim I would make about any technique or equipment or scientific knowledge as relates to dentistry would always be followed by the same response and question, "How do you know?"

Lest you think that this is a trick that he uses in argument and conversation, you need to know that this is a question he asks of himself as well. This was demonstrated to me when I was in dental school, where my father teaches. He was the instructor for one of the courses that I took and at the time he had been practicing dentistry for more than 25 years. I have always been impressed by the fact that, while I was in school, he constantly asked me questions about what new material I had learned, and he was always interested in what I had to say. With all of his experience, what could he possibly learn from me? Even so, he asked. Often, he would incorporate this new information into his practice. You see, he was being responsible. He was searching for truth and then doing the right thing. He was always thinking and acting on purpose. By searching for truth he was asking himself, "How do I know that what I'm doing today is the best for my patients? How do I know that the knowledge that I have is up-to-date?" Asking himself "How do you know?" led him to asking me what I had learned, and then incorporating that learning into his teaching and practice of dentistry. He is my model of a professional. He is my mentor for studying and practicing dentistry.

Are you a professional in your area of expertise? Are you up-to-date with your knowledge? Are you dedicated to a lifetime of learning? Are you climbing up a "ladder of learning?" Remember, you can win or *learn*. If you learn, you almost always win. Basing your behavior and your actions on that learning empowers you to actualize your potential and achieve extraordinary results and therefore to achieve happiness. But how do we know our learning is accurate? How do we know if we are truly enlightened? Let's investigate my father's favorite question "How do you know?" I call this "Knowing 101."

We began addressing this issue in Chapter 2. There we discussed the lessons of learning as they applied to the question "Why me?" Those lessons also apply to the question "How do you know?"

Lesson 1: I will never know for sure. Absolute truth exists, but we will never know it absolutely. Whatever method we use to know things, it will never give us absolute knowledge. While there exists within each of us a fundamental consciousness that the universe makes sense, that there is some absolute truth, we cannot know that truth for sure. As we have explained, this is related to the existence of uncertainty and pluralism, as well as God's withdrawal and hiding of his absolute truth. In other words, whatever method we decide to use to know whatever we wish to know will be imperfect in some way. After applying that methodology we will still not know for sure and we will still make mistakes. But, the flipside remains in place. Because we cannot know for sure, we have freedom. In this case it is freedom to choose our methodology of knowing, of learning, of gaining understanding of this universe. This raises the question, "What is the best methodology for learning?" This was addressed in Lesson 2.

Lesson 2: I want to know anyway. Even though no methodology exists that will lead us to perfect knowledge, I want to use the best of the various imperfect methods of learning. I want to take responsibility. In my quest to serve others, I must gain knowledge and wisdom so that I can make better (never perfect) decisions, thinking and acting on purpose. The tool I have devised for this process I call *The Ladder of Learning*. As you climb The Ladder of Learning you achieve higher levels of understanding, leading to better choices, better results, with more joy and inner peace-happiness. *Using the Ladder of Learning empowers us to be able to learn any time that we lose.* We need not remain as powerless victims. We can turn any loss into a victory.

Lesson 3: I want to know my purpose. Yet, "How do you know?" How do you know your purpose? In the next chapter we will apply the methodology of The Ladder of Learning to discovering your purpose, the meaning and values important to you in your life. I call this The Timeless Values Connection. For now, let's investigate The Ladder of Learning in detail.

The Ladder of Learning

The ultimate purpose of The Ladder of Learning is to help people reach higher levels of happiness. The ladder consists of a series of steps, or tools, leading to higher levels of understanding. The decisions, actions, and results one achieves are based on the level of understanding that one has achieved on the ladder. Climbing the ladder leads to better decisions, better actions, better results, and, over time, more happiness.

Stimulus and Response

Stimulus ⟶ **Response**

Stimulus and response is where we start. Stephen Covey says that there is a space between stimulus and response. The key to our growth and our happiness is how we use that space. "Between stimulus and response man has the freedom to choose."[33] The key to a better life is making better choices. The choices we make lead us to take action, and these actions lead to consequences in the real world. If we want better results in the real world, we need to make better choices inside our minds. The Ladder of Learning system was created to help people respond to any stimulus in life in the best way possible.

At any moment in your life you can experience a stimulus from reality—from outside of you. A stimulus is something that leads to action. The question is, how do we know what is the best action, what our response should be? First, we need to understand reality and the individual stimulus in particular. We thus need to understand what is happening outside of us in reality. Second, what happens on the outside is processed on the inside. We must process the information (the stimulus) that came from outside of us, inside of us. Understanding those processes can help us make better decisions. There are levels of understanding, and the higher the level we achieve, the better our choices, our response, and our results will be.

Level 1 Response

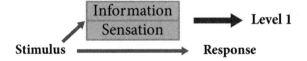

The first level of stimulus and response is reflex. Do we have any choice at the level of reflex? Probably not. Certainly we do not have the kind of choice that one has higher up on the Ladder of Learning. In fact, what we have here is preprocessed information. So, for example, when a doctor tests your reflexes and taps you on your knee, you receive a stimulus. A signal goes through the nervous system into the spinal cord. It does not go up to the level of the brain. It simply circles around from the sensory into the motor system and results in a response, which is the motion of your leg. This is a reflex. Have you chosen this? No. Certainly you have not chosen at the level of your brain. You have not chosen at the level of knowledge. This is a Level 1 response to a stimulus. Level 1 is the level of no choice. You respond to a stimulus with a reflex.

Some individuals, at times, operate at this level. This is a level of victimhood. A victim responds without processing his or her problems, without referencing to thinking and higher emotional levels, and without referencing to knowledge, reason, wisdom, and certainly not to the soul. They have become simply an object—a victim. Through their victimization they have limited themselves to Level 1 understanding and response.

Let's follow two possible real life examples of climbing the Ladder of Learning. One example will be located at work, while the other example will be at home.

Jim is a general dentist with his own private practice. He has two kids in college. With the downturn in the economy, issues with insurance companies, and with many of his patients out of work, he is facing some serious financial issues. His staff is feeling the pressure and work is no longer fun. Mrs. Collins is sitting in his dental chair complaining about the new crown that he had just recently placed. Jim had to work exceedingly hard due to the particular difficulty of her case. He had previously warned her that this problem could be expected. He also previously told her that she would need to see a specialist if the problem arose. She seems to have forgotten any previous conversation, and is blaming him for the problem. Jim is feeling totally victimized and walks through the rest of his day mindlessly, working as if using only reflexes. This is a Level 1 response at work.

Kate is a stay-at-home mom whose husband has recently been laid off work. She loves being home with the kids, but may need to return to the workplace. Kate is on her way home, having just received a diagnosis of breast cancer. At this point, Kate is devastated. Her first response to the stimulus of cancer is to think of herself as a "cancer victim." As such, all of her responses are at the level of being a victim—Level 1 responses. She simply goes through the motions of life, numbed by her situation.

To move out of victimhood and to win, one must learn. Jim and Kate must enroll in Learning 101. They must learn to accept responsibility and use the gifts given to each of them to make better, more informed, more knowledgeable, and wiser decisions leading to better responses. They must climb the Ladder of Learning.

Let's move on to the next level where we take information and sensation and process them.

Level 2 Response

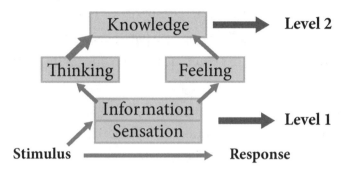

At this level we engage the brain in thinking and feeling. This processing of information and sensation through our thinking and our feeling leads to a level of understanding best described as knowledge. Early in the processing of information and sensation, we focus on feeling and look for the emotion that comes from the stimulus. Feeling occurs at a lower level of the brain than thinking. Feeling is an animal level brain function known as the pleasure pain principle. We respond to any stimulus with feelings of pleasure or pain. We can use those feelings to make Level 2 decisions. Generally, we will find ways of responding to stimuli that increase pleasure or decrease pain.

As human beings we must take care to use thinking over feeling. This is especially true when asking the question "Why me?" This is a question usually asked after an emotionally traumatic experience (stimulus). The initial response that we have to that stimulus is highly emotional, as we feel overwhelmed by the pain of our problem. Responding on a purely emotional level can lead to awful responses. Crimes of passion are examples of such responses. On a more practical level, often your child or your customer can drive you into an emotional frenzy that you hide beneath your calm exterior.

Let's return to Jim and Kate. Jim could respond to his patient Mrs. Collins with an emotional outburst. He could lash out at her for all the issues that he is facing. He could also take out his frustrations on his staff, or bring them home. Similarly, Kate could respond with her own emotional outburst. She could blame her husband for the cancer because of the stress he has been giving her by being off work. She could take it out on her kids. Or, she could take it on herself by blaming herself for the cancer and trying to cry it away. None of these emotional responses would lead to being happy in the short term or happiness in the long term.

To win in this situation, you must go up the ladder of learning using thinking in addition to your feelings, and respond using knowledge. You must understand how and why you feel the way that you do in those circumstances. The feeling itself is legitimate. The feeling itself is a messenger. The feeling itself is giving you a signal that you need to change something. You must think about your feelings. You must use knowledge from thinking over knowledge from feeling to decide your response. You must then use your knowledge to manage your feelings. At that point feelings can be used to empower us with the emotion, energy, and desire to act on our knowledge.

What is knowledge?

Knowledge is an organized body of information. *It is the result of investigating, studying, processing, and organizing information and sensations.* Knowledge is a state of knowing that can be general or specific. General knowledge combines all particular subjects, thus it is the sum of what is known. Specific knowledge is familiarity with or expertise in a particular subject or branch of learning. Examples of these subjects include philosophy, science, religion, technology, economics, ethics, sports, cooking, travel, mathematics, literature (stories), and politics. Notice that subjects can cover every area of human endeavor. Each branch of learning has its own systems, rules, and methodology for learning. When facing any stimulus, experience, or issue, we can use our knowledge in that field to make a Level 2, knowledgeable response.

Even though our response is knowledgeable, we cannot find or use perfect knowledge. Steven Goldberg, professor at Lehigh University in the departments of philosophy and history in his tape series, *Science Wars: What Scientists Know and How They Know It,* notes that there has been, "A 2400 year old war in Western philosophy over the meaning of the terms knowledge, truth, reason, and reality."[34] Two positions exist:

1. Knowledge as "**Truth**" about reality.
2. Knowledge as **strong beliefs** about experiences.

Plato and his followers understand knowledge to refer to "that about which one cannot be wrong. Beliefs or opinions refer to that about which one could be wrong. That's why they're called beliefs and opinions. Knowledge is not a matter of belief or opinion. Knowledge is what is true."[35]

The second position is maintained by the Sophists. They "were primarily concerned with action. They were concerned with making decisions in the real world, real life situations. For the Sophists the word *knowledge* referred to a species of belief. It referred to those beliefs that are most strongly held in a society at a particular time."[36]

Plato's view is that knowledge is universal (true for all time and space), necessary (cannot be otherwise), and certain (we can be sure that it is true). The Sophists' view is that knowledge comes from experience and therefore it is always particular (specific to one experience in a particular time and place), is always contingent (dependent on assumptions that are not themselves known to be true), and is always probable (uncertainty exists—we cannot know for sure). Which view is correct? Yes. Again we face a paradox. To understand and resolve this paradox, we must take a deeper look at the concepts of knowledge, experience, and reality.

This dispute can be seen today in science. Modern science wants to have it both ways. "Modern science prides itself on being empirical and experimental, but at the same time, at the end of all the experimentation comes a universal, necessary, and certain theory." Goldman asks, "What is the object of scientific knowledge? Is it reality...something which is out there which we do not experience but we know is the cause of our experience? Or is the object of scientific knowledge experience...an account of experience that we accept because it works."[37] Our intuition is that what we mean by reality is something changeless. Yet scientific knowledge changes all the time. At the same time, scientific knowledge seems be more than simply a description of our experiences.

Goldman presents an excellent resolution to this problem. Separate from and in addition to the terms *reality* and *experience,* he introduces the term **actuality.** The relationship between ordinary experience and reality is very controversial and emotional. If we substitute the word actuality and say scientific theories are about actualities, not reality, our understanding is improved.

What are scientific actualities? **Scientific actualities are interim conceptions of objects defined by scientists using the scientific method** (experimentation using observation and instrumentation, along with inductive reasoning). Scientific actualities include such objects as the sun, the earth, atoms, genes, and black holes. Ask a scientist what is real and the answer will be particles, forces, and fields etc., in other words actualities defined by science. To the scientist, an actuality is real. Scientists see those objects differently from the way non-scientists perceive them. A geologist sees the earth as a specific scientific object, an actuality, with a superficial layer of crust over moving tectonic plates and a molten core. To the geologist this scientific actuality is more real than ordinary experience. However, as scientific methodology and understanding progresses, what is "known" about the Earth as an actuality will change over time. Actualities, as opposed to reality, can change over time. Reality is a realm of timelessness; universal, necessary, and certain truth. It is what is really out there independent of our experiences. That does not change over time; therefore science never gets to that reality. **Lesson #1 applies here: absolute truth exists (Plato's Reality), but we can never know it absolutely (the Sophists position). Paradoxically, to some extent both Plato and the Sophists are correct.**

This leads us to lesson #2: We want to know "truth" anyway. We are engaged in a quest for the truth, a process in which we aspire to know. Here we are not after absolute truth (Reality) but rather we're after "Actualities." These actualities are more than experience alone (Sophists) but less than absolute truth (Plato). Actualities change over time as scientists change their paradigms. Scientific paradigms are the eyeglasses through which scientists see reality. Paradigms are theories, mapping criteria, and rules that give us the actualities. Scientific theories map empirical experience (experiments) not onto some ultimate and inexperienceable "Reality", but onto actualities. Actualities are our maps of the territory (reality). Through experimentation we test our maps, our pictures of these actualities. We can test the correspondence of these actualities to our experience.

Science is the study of the natural world, of what is and how it works. The power of using science is that it increases our understanding of physical reality. It gives us an ability to predict experiences and it gives us some power and control over nature. Add in technological scientific advances, and we can understand how science empowers us to respond better in a physical, materialistic sense to any stimulus or experience.

Science is not the only source of actualities; it's not the only story that we tell about our experiences. In fact, every area of knowledge tells us different stories about experience in different ways using different tools that create actualities unique to that area of study. Let's look quickly at two other examples of specific areas of knowledge: philosophy and religion. Philosophy studies how we know what we know. "How do you know?" is, first of all, a philosophical question. What is philosophy? Jeffrey Kasser, Professor at North Carolina State University, quotes his teacher David Hills: "Philosophy is the art of asking questions that come naturally to children using methods that come naturally to lawyers."[38]

In other words, philosophers ask big questions, turning the big questions into smaller, more manageable ones, using evidence and logic along the way. With a better understanding of how we think, using philosophical actualities, we can make better choices and responses to our problems.

There are five types of philosophical questions:
1. Ontological: What is? What exists? What is real?
2. Epistemological: How do you know?
3. Ethical: How should we act?
4. Political: How should we act together?
5. Meaning and Purpose: Why are we here?

Philosophical actualities are interim answers to those five questions. Philosophical actualities include objects and ideas. Ask a philosopher what is real and her answer will be based on her philosophical school of thought. To a Platonic philosopher, the metaphysical (one philosophical actuality) is real.

Religious actualities are interim conceptions of objects, ideas, and other aspects defined by theologians and clergy using religious/spiritual methods.

Religious knowledge has four aspects:
1. A narrative, which is a story.
2. A system of beliefs or doctrine.
3. A set of rituals.
4. A system of ethics.

Interestingly, when one compares religions, the higher up one goes on the list, the greater the differences between religions become. Conversely, the lower one goes on the list, the more religions resemble each other. Each religion has a unique story. Theological differences are what define the borders of religions. Although some rituals are common between religions, clearly there are major ritual differences. Only when we come to a system of ethics do we find broad agreements between religions.

Stephen Prothero in his book, *God Is Not One*, agrees, "The world's religious rivals do converge when it comes to ethics, but they diverge sharply on doctrine, ritual, mythology, experience, and law...and in some cases religious differences move adherence to fight and to kill."[39] He goes on to point out:

> *"What the world's religions share is not so much a finish line as a starting point. And where they begin is with this simple observation: Something is wrong with the world...They part company, however, when it comes to stating just what has gone wrong, and they diverge sharply when they move from diagnosing the human problem to prescribing how to solve it. Christians see sin as the problem and salvation from sin as the religious goal. Buddhists see suffering as the problem and liberation from suffering as the religious goal. If practitioners of the world's religions are all mountain*

climbers, then they are on very different mountains, climbing very different peaks, and using very different tools and techniques in their ascents."[40]

Ultimately God may be one, but there are many different ways that humans play out God's unity. In other words, there are many different religious actualities.

While different religions ask different questions and provide different answers to those questions, all religions ask about our human condition. Why are we here, what is our purpose, and how are we to live as human beings? People throughout the world today are turning to religion for answers. It is often found in regions of conflict. Yet at the same time religion is a source of values, a source for solving problems, and a source for finding purpose and meaning leading to healing, joy, and inner peace—happiness.

Ask a theologian what is real and his answer will be God, the soul, miracles, the power of prayer, etc. To a religious person, these religious actualities are real.

Thus science is one source of knowledge, philosophy is another, and religion is yet another. There are many others. In our quest for truth, we do not get reality but rather we get actualities. As interim concepts, actualities change over time. Is there, however, a source for us to find timeless truths, timeless values?

Now we return to our paradox. Which view is correct? Is it Plato's view of knowledge as "**Truth**" about reality or is it the Sophists view of knowledge as **strong beliefs** about experiences? Yes. In some ways both are correct in some ways both are wrong.

There is a higher reality, a metaphysical reality, God's reality; Plato was correct on that account. Universal truth exists. However, in tapping into God's knowing we get only actualities, never reality itself. On that account the Sophists were right. Our knowledge consists of strong interim beliefs about our experiences, a series of actualities. We need a method to tap into timeless truths, God's knowing. Is there a way to integrate all of the different parts of knowledge, all of the different actualities, into a greater whole? Can we form a mosaic of knowledge, giving us a metaphysical level of knowing? These are issues, problems, and questions that go beyond Level 2, the level of knowledge. To deal with these issues, we must move on to Levels 3 and 4.

Before we move on let's see what Jim and Kate are doing at Level 2. Jim has decided to move beyond the emotional level. Thinking about his problems, he realizes that each one falls into some area of knowledge. By learning more about each area, he can use that knowledge to solve problems in that particular area. By acting on that knowledge, he can improve his life at work. He can use science to achieve better results in his clinical dentistry. He can use psychology with patients and with his team to understand and relate to them better. He can use religious knowledge to understand some of the problems he is facing at work, the problems of being human, and help him to find his purpose. In each area he uses the best knowledge of the day, he uses actualities. These actualities lead to the best practices (yet never perfect practices).

Similarly, Kate has moved beyond a purely emotional response at home. She is no longer a cancer victim. She is someone who suffers from cancer and is looking to heal that suffering. She has been searching for knowledge about cancer by surfing the Web. She has begun reading books covering all aspects of cancer. Some books are scientific, some are self-help books, and some are religious/spiritual texts. She still has deep issues about her cancer, but she is now beginning to understand what she is facing. Her cancer is an actuality that she refines over time. With that knowledge, she is feeling better prepared for what lies ahead.

Level 3 Response

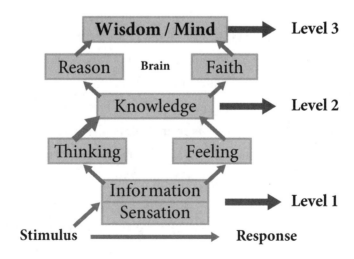

The next level involves integrating your knowledge and bringing it to a higher level of understanding, which is the level of wisdom. For you to understand this next level, I must introduce you to something that I call:

The Mosaic of Knowledge

General knowledge combines all particular subjects and thus it is the sum of what is known. The sum of knowledge is like a puzzle. Each area of study and each branch of learning will give us different part of the puzzle. But none of them alone will give us the whole puzzle—the whole truth. Many of you already know the ancient tale of blind men describing parts of an elephant. The blind man who feels a leg says it is a pillar; the one who feels the tail says it is a rope; the one who feels the trunk says it is a tree branch; the one who feels the ear says it is a hand fan; the one who feels the belly says it is a wall; and the one who feels the tusk says it is a solid pipe. They bicker about what this "thing" could "really" be. One point of this ancient tale is that each blind man is clearly wrong if he claims to have the whole truth about the elephant. However, even in his description of his own area of study, the one part of the elephant in which he has some expertise, he has failed to reach the truth, the actual reality of that part.

What we have here can be described as a *mosaic of knowledge*. A mosaic is a picture or decoration made of small, usually colored, pieces of inlaid stone, glass, etc. It is another example of a whole-parts-whole process. The artist has in mind a whole, finished, picture. She creates that whole picture, however, with individual pictures, individual parts, and individual pieces of the mosaic. Each piece in itself can have its own beauty and meaning. Understanding each piece alone is a challenge. However, when each individual picture is put together with all the other pictures a new picture emerges. Emerging from the parts is a new whole—a whole that is greater than the sum of its parts. This thought was expressed by the 13th century Sufi teacher Jalaluddin Rumi:"You think because you understand *one* you must understand *two*, because one and one makes two. But you must also understand *and*."[41]

Remember in Chapter 3 we used a watch as an example to explain whole-parts-whole? If we take it apart piece by piece and place all the pieces on a table, what would we call that? Certainly it's not a watch, because it doesn't work. You could call it the parts of a watch. You could call it a broken watch. What happens if you put it back together? When all the parts operate together, a new property emerges (***and***) that cannot be found from the parts of the watch alone. The emergent property is that a whole, operating watch that can tell time. Actually, the watch does not tell time. We tell the time on the watch and, in so doing, we add meaning and purpose to this world.

Just as one cannot separate parts from the whole and gain full knowledge, one cannot separate, isolate, or focus on only one aspect of our human existence (for example, science, philosophy, religion, or spirituality) *and gain full knowledge of our universe.* As human beings, we will never see the complete mosaic of objective reality. However, using the concept of the mosaic of knowledge there is much that we can learn.

Using a mosaic of knowledge emergent properties arise, such as wisdom and mind. You cannot predict their existence from the parts alone. Only when the parts are combined together into a whole do these properties emerge.

Here is another example. Put two masses in proximity and gravity emerges. You cannot predict that mass can lead to gravity by looking at mass alone. So too, just looking at the molecules of matter in no way allows you to predict that from that matter life could emerge. In fact, you have many laws of thermodynamics (laws of entropy, disorder) that would speak against even the possibility of the emergence of life. And yet, unpredictably, out of matter emerges life. Similarly, when the parts of the brain are put together, the mind emerges. You could not predict from the brain itself that a mind can emerge. Nor could you predict that from the mosaic of knowledge wisdom would emerge. Emergent properties are more than the simple properties observable in the parts. Where does that extra come from?

It is possible that emergent properties arise from the metaphysical dimension. What we may be seeing here, potentially, is the hidden face of God. Emergent properties may come from a dimension outside our space-time box, one that cannot be directly observed in our dimensions, yet its effects can be seen here. This is similar to energy. Have you ever seen energy? No, but you have seen its effects. So it is with a higher dimension hidden, yet present. It is here in that metaphysical dimension where mind emerges from the brain and wisdom emerges from the mosaic of knowledge.

In the diagram below please note the line of demarcation just below Level 3. It is a separation between the physical and metaphysical aspects of the ladder of learning. Everything below the line occurs in the space-time (ST) box, the physical world. Everything above the line exists in a metaphysical state.

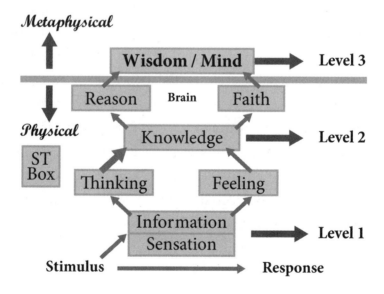

To get to the third level, which is mindful wisdom, you must use reason and faith. Reason is a wonderful tool for learning. However, there are some things that we seek to understand that are beyond reason alone. For those items we need to have faith. We must make assumptions at some level on things that we cannot show to be true or false just yet. We must start with the belief that our assumptions in those situations are probably true. That is to say we have Faith that they are true. With faith we are going beyond the physical brain and engaging in mindfulness (notice in the diagram that the brain is on the physical side while the mind is on the metaphysical side of the line of demarcation).

The mind is metaphysical consciousness. It consists of an awareness that goes beyond the physical properties of the brain itself. This awareness of the metaphysical, this Faith in the truth of propositions that cannot be supported by reason alone, empowers our connection to wisdom. To understand wisdom, we must first learn more about faith and reason as they apply to science and religion. We will then see how that leads to unified understanding and to wisdom.

In trying to answer the question "How do you know?" Science and Religion *both* focus on Faith (beliefs and assumptions) as well as Reason (logic and rationality). There are some who claim that religion works by faith while science works by reason and that this is the key difference between the two. This is inaccurate. Science must often depend upon faith statements, assumptions that are unprovable, in addition to its use of reason.

There is faith in science that:

* The universe is sensible.
* The universe has order.
  * There are laws.
  * There is rationality.
  * There is organization.
* The universe is accessible to our rational human minds.
* The laws of physics apply everywhere and at all times.

In addition, Steven Goldberg notes that there are four faith assumptions of science that exist from Medieval and Renaissance times:

1. The task of natural philosophy (science) is to explain natural phenomena in terms of their (material) **causes**.
2. When explaining natural phenomena, nature must be treated as a closed system (ST box). There can be no use of supernatural explanations. Natural phenomenon can be explained as the effects of natural causal agents only.
3. Knowledge of nature must be based on direct **experience** or repeatable **experiments**, not textual statements by **authorities**.
4. Mathematics is a "language" for describing natural phenomena.[42]

While seemingly unarguably true, these assumptions cannot be deduced from experience. We could be wrong about them, but since we cannot know the whole future for sure, we must make these assumptions. They allow us to do our work in science.

Similarly, theology relies significantly on the exercise of reason. Great philosophical works have come from religious thinkers such as Avicenna (Islamic 980–1037), Maimonides (Jewish 1135–1204), and Thomas Aquinas (Christian 1225–1274). Anyone familiar with the Jewish Talmud knows that many of its legal and philosophical issues are resolved using reason. The Talmud emphasizes the use of logic and reason in studying the law as a religious activity in and of itself.

Let's return to our question "How do you know?" Even when we ask the question "Why" we must follow up with the question "How do you know?" What method of learning and what method of knowing will you apply? What evidence will you collect and how will you collect it? Let's apply science/materialism and religion/spirituality to the question "Why?"

To begin, let's try an exercise to help us figure this out. What would you expect to happen if I held a pen in my hand and then let go? Of course you would expect it to fall. We can do a scientific experiment and see if that is true. If you try this at home, you will notice that the pen falls every time. (Please do this carefully because scientific experiments can be dangerous at home.)

Now let me ask you a question. **Why** did that pen fall? Did I hear you say gravity? Wrong! Sorry, but this was a bit of a trick question. The trick comes from the fact that most of us do not know the proper epistemological use of the word "*Why.*" To understand this, first understand that gravity is the answer to a "**how**" question or a "**what**" question. If you ask the question, "**How** did that pen fall?" The answer I would give you is that it fell at 9.8 meters per second squared due to gravitational force. *How* did it fall? The answer is gravity.

Another scientific question would be, "**What** is it about that pen that whenever I let it go, it falls?" The answer would be that the pen has mass and the Earth has mass. Masses attract and we call that attraction gravity. Gravity is a name that describes *what is* and explains *how it works*. Gravity in no way explains *why* the pen fell.

Why did the object fall is a metaphysical, not a physical question. Why did it fall asks for what purpose did that object fall? What is the meaning behind the fact that it fell? What is the value of it falling? We could ask "Why" did it fall and "Why" is there gravity? We could answer that gravity is a metaphor for attraction—for love. This would be a poetic metaphysical answer. We could also answer that the meaning, purpose, and value of gravity is for us to exist. Without gravity our parts would be floating throughout the universe. There would be no physical world as we know it. We would have no chance to actualize our purpose here. 'Why' questions are religious-spiritual-metaphysical questions.

When a scientist asks why the object fell she is asking what I call a why question with a small "w." Why questions with a small "w" are really asking how and what. These are the questions upon which science focuses. A scientist might pose the question, "Why did the ball roll down the hill?" What she means here is, "*How* did the ball roll down the hill?" Or "*What* caused the ball to roll down the hill?"

On the other hand, why questions with a large "W" are asking deep spiritual why questions. Spiritually, we may ask, "Why do we exist," or "Why do we suffer?" Those deeper questions are only answered metaphysically using religion or philosophy, never physically using science.

Science and religion are two paradigms, two tools, two methods, with two sets of actualities and two different perspectives for describing the same reality. Science is the study of the natural world, of what physically "is". Religion/spirituality is a study of what exists metaphysically, of what "ought to be". Science only deals with the ordinary dimensions of this world inside our space-time box (ST box). Religion deals with an extraordinary dimension outside our ST box and its effects inside the box.

+ Science describes the physical, but hints of the metaphysical. Religion focuses on the metaphysical and its role in the physical.
+ While Science tells us *how,* Religion tells us *why.*
+ Science focuses on *what,* whereas Religion focuses on *what for.*

+ Science is descriptive, describing our acts, while Religion is prescriptive, telling us how we ought to act.

+ Science focuses on observable facts and Religion focuses on values.

+ Science focuses on physical power, i.e., the laws of nature. Religion focuses on spiritual power—love.

+ Science focuses its study on the parts in order to understand the whole, while Religion focuses its study on the whole to give meaning to the parts.

+ Science and Religion *both* focus on beliefs and assumptions (faith) as well as logic and rationality (reason).

+ When answering the question "How do you know?" Science uses the scientific method and Religion uses sacred texts as well as inner and outer revelation.

> + Science uses the "Book of Nature" (how things came to be).

> + Religion uses the "Book of the Bible" (why things came to be).

If I walk off a building, science can describe exactly *what* will happen to me. Science is factual and descriptive. *Should* I walk off the building? Science can never answer that question. It is a prescriptive, values laden question. Religion discusses how we ought to act and what acts are prescribed, both of which deal with our values. To science, the molecules in a table have the same value as the molecules in my brain. Religion/spirituality empowers me to judge the value of my brain as being greater than that of a table. Should I walk off the building or not is a spiritual not a scientific question.

So, which of these two paradigms gets us closer to truth? Is it science/materialism or religion/spirituality? Which of these paradigms should Jim and Kate use to obtain better results for their individual situations? My answer is that they will need to use both. At work, Jim will need to use the *mosaic of knowledge*. As a dental professional, Jim must combine his knowledge of science (*what* to do for his patient and *how* to do it) with his knowledge about values (*why* he should or should not do it for this particular patient).

When we combine reason **and** faith and apply them to the mosaic of knowledge, the result is wisdom. Wisdom allows us to see that the individual parts of the mosaic blend together into an integrated whole. As a whole person Jim is facing troubles at the office and at home. Which is more important? Of course home is more important, but home does not exist by itself. What happens at work deeply affects what happens at home. That is why your path to happiness is at work **and** at home.

Similarly Kate moves on to fighting to cure her cancer at Level 3. Is this fight about work or about home? Is her fight on a scientific or spiritual/metaphysical level? The answer to both questions is "Yes!" Once again we face a paradox, but now we can see that this paradox involves wisdom.

As previously stated, a paradox is two seemingly conflicting or contradictory statements or concepts that on a deeper level simultaneously seem to be true. How can this be so? How can this be wisdom? You may be familiar with the wave particle duality of light. Light can be understood using the physics of waves or it can be understood using the physics of particles. These are two different ways of looking at light. Which one is true? The amazing answer from physics is that both ways are correct. Light is a wavicle! It is best defined as both particle and wave.

Science has discovered that a fundamental part of the nature of our universe, our reality, is paradox. Neil Bohr, one of the pioneers in quantum physics is said to have put it this way: **"The opposite of a correct statement is a false statement. But the opposite of a profound truth is another profound truth."** [43]

What does he mean? If you grabbed a chair and stated, "This is a chair." That would be a simple correct statement. The opposite of that statement would be, "This is a table." That would be a falsehood. So the opposite of a simple truth is a falsehood. With simple, opposite parts, we can keep them as distinct separate entities. Being simple and separate, we can apply the term true to one and false to the other. However, if we were to state that we are physical beings, the opposite statement would be that we are spiritual beings. Well, which one is it? Things get messier in this case because we are dealing with profound concepts that overlap each other. It is then that the whole-parts-whole issues come into play.

You may remember from an earlier chapter that originally all reality and all concepts were one, whole, and unified. At creation and/or birth unity breaks up and we live amongst the parts, partial truths. **Profound truths overlap in our existence.** *This leads to the paradox that two seemingly opposite parts are connected to some harmonious unity on some level.* Particles and waves both describe a single part—a photon of light. The opposite of a profound truth (light is made up of particles) is very often another profound truth (light is made up of waves).

So, are we physical beings or are we spiritual beings? Are we rational beings or are we emotional beings? Are we good beings or are we evil beings? Are the Sophists correct or is Plato correct when it comes to knowledge? *Are we scientists or theologians?* The answer to all of these questions is "Yes." Just as light is both a particle and wave, depending on how we choose to observe it, so too science and religion are both valid descriptions of our full reality, depending on how we choose to observe them.

Understanding these paradoxes leads to wisdom and better decision-making. *Wisdom is integrated, balanced, and harmonious understanding.* As Rabbi Bunam said, "everyone must have two pockets, so that he can reach into one or the other, according to his needs. In his right pocket are to be the words: 'For my sake the world was created,' and in his left: 'I am Earth and ashes.'"[44] To make wise decisions, one must realize the paradox of human existence. We must realize that we are both good and evil, that we are physical and metaphysical, that we have a brain and we also have a mind. We must also understand that wisdom requires combining reason and faith and integrating them with knowledge.

So then, what is wisdom?

+ Wisdom is consciousness.

+ Wisdom is recognizing the existence of the metaphysical.

+ Wisdom is making a connection with the world out there.

+ Wisdom is the ability to make extraordinary choices.

+ Wisdom is a lifetime of accumulated understanding and insight, as well as knowledge.

+ Wisdom is both artisanship and professionalism.

+ Wisdom integrates physical and metaphysical understanding.

+ Wisdom is taking proper, meaningful, and purposeful action.

+ Wisdom is choosing appropriate values and acting on those values.

+ Wisdom is the use of practical principles that control and direct human living at its highest and best.

Wisdom – Mind - Consciousness

Wisdom is, however, even more than what has been listed above. According to Gerald Schroeder in his book, *God According to God*, wisdom and mind are very special entities. To get his point, let's go right to the beginning. The first page of the King James Version of the Bible famously opens (Genesis, 1:1):

"In the beginning God created the heaven and the earth."

Interestingly, Schroeder points out, "In the beginning" is a mistranslation of the first word of the Hebrew Bible. The Hebrew compound word Breisheet translates to "in the beginning of." But there is no object in Hebrew text following the word "of." It would read, "In the beginning of, God created the heavens and the earth." This doesn't make sense—in the beginning of what? So the Greek and the Latin versions, and eventually the King James Version, deleted the word "of." A better translation would be "With a first cause (Breisheet) God created the heavens and the earth." What was that first cause? The answer comes from the 2100 year old Jerusalem translation of the Bible into Aramaic, a sister language of Hebrew. **"With wisdom God created the heavens and the earth."**[45] Wisdom, or mind, is a totally metaphysical emanation from the creator, yet it yielded the Big Bang creation of the physical universe within which we dwell.

Wisdom is the substrate of every particle of the world and is most evident in the brains and minds of humans as we puzzle over these thoughts.

A single consciousness, an all encompassing wisdom, pervades the universe. All existence is the expression of this wisdom. Every particle, every being, from atom to human, appears to have a level of information within it—a level of conscious wisdom. Where does this conscious wisdom come from? At first glance, there is no hint of it in science, in the laws of nature that govern the interactions among the basic particles composing all matter. Religion/spirituality, on the other hand, sees all existence as emerging from God's transcendent metaphysical wisdom. Universal consciousness (mind) is the manifestation of that wisdom.

Remember that God created the universe by withdrawing. When he withdrew, however, he did leave some of his wisdom in every part of the universe. If we substitute the word information for wisdom, then religion/spirituality begins to sound like quantum physics. In this way science is beginning to understand the relationship between the physical and the spiritual—the unity underlying all existence.

"Wait a minute," you say. "This table here in front of me is physical, solid stuff. See, I can knock on it (knocking sounds heard). This is not metaphysical!"

Oh really? That table is made up of atoms. Atoms are made up of a nucleus in the center and electrons orbiting around the nucleus. If we were to enlarge the nucleus to about the size of a fist (about 4 inches) the electrons can be *4 miles away!* That seemingly "solid" table is made up of 99.9999999999999 percent **empty space!** Then why doesn't my hand fly through the table when I knock on it? That is because the space is not totally empty. It is filled with energy. Electromagnetic energy holds the atoms and the table together. What is energy? It is electromagnetic force, a force field. What is a force field? It is described by a mathematical equation. In other words it is just a bunch of information. Your hand is knocking against information! Information is not very solid at all.

Most of us have heard of Albert Einstein's famous equation, $E = MC^2$ (Energy = Mass times the speed of light squared). Notice that the formula equates energy and matter (mass). Energy and matter are thus two different forms of the same "stuff." To understand this, consider the three states of water (H_2O). H_2O can be found frozen as ice, liquid as water, and a gas as steam. It is all the same stuff, just in different states. By applying heat energy, we can change the state of the water from frozen to liquid to gas. By cooling, we can change the state of the water from gas to liquid to frozen solid. It's all the same H_2O, just in different states. The same is true for information, energy, and matter. Matter turns out to be nothing more than "frozen," condensed energy, while energy is condensed Information. In fact, the amount of condensation of the energy is represented by C^2 in the formula. That energy is a huge amount—it is the speed of light squared. That is why one can change a small amount of matter into a huge amount of energy released in an atom bomb.

We have established that matter is condensed energy and energy is information. That is the understanding of science today.

Once again we encounter paradigms, actualities (to you that object is a solid table, to a physicist it is an electromagnetic field), and paradox (solid emptiness). We must be close to the metaphysical. Emerging from "solid" matter is energy. Emerging from energy is information. Is it possible that emerging from information is wisdom? Could it be the wisdom that "created" the universe with a Big Bang? Gerald Schroeder has taught me that it is not a very large leap to assume that information comes from metaphysical wisdom. The source of that metaphysical wisdom is, of course, the Power and Loving Greater Than Ourselves—God.

From God's viewpoint the transitions appear as follows:
God→metaphysical→wisdom→information→energy→matter

At each step God withdraws and hides a bit more until he is virtually unnoticeable in ordinary matter, leading to the possibility that there is only scientific materialism.

From our human viewpoint the transitions appear as follows:

Matter→energy→information→<u>wisdom</u>→metaphysical→God

At each step we notice a new emergent property. From our point of view, everything seems to be emerging from matter. That's because we experience our universe as only material parts. It is hard for us to see the emergent whole. It is especially hard for us to "see" the hidden God. That is why we should listen, and not look, for God. God is immaterial, beyond the metaphysical, and cannot be seen. We must listen for God's voice as we shall learn in the final section of this chapter.

The idea that a universal consciousness, emerging from this wisdom, might be present in what we habitually refer to as inert matter finds support in a range of scientific data. For example, if you bring a proton of positive spin close to a second proton, the second proton will assume a negative spin. Now separate them so that it would take a long time for communication to occur. Expose the first proton to a field that changes its spin from positive to negative and instantaneously the second proton will change to a positive spin. It is as if each particle is simultaneously aware of the other's action at the instant of the action.

Another example comes from, of all things, a newer concept of dental decay. Before you decide to skip ahead, thinking that any discussion of dental decay cannot turn out well for you, let me explain. Not only am I a motivational speaker and a former practicing dentist, but I have spoken all over the world on treating tooth decay with medicine instead of a drill. A lesion on a tooth is formed by the biofilm on top of the tooth. Tooth biofilm is what we call dental plaque. Bacteria are present in dental plaque biofilm. It is acid from those bacteria that cause tooth decay lesions. Using medicines we can cause positive changes in the biofilm helping to control the disease. However, the bacteria resist our efforts. Using biochemical messengers they signal each other. As a result of this communication they change their genetics, their structure and their defense system. They have an organized response.

The bacterial biofilm has "mindful," lifelike characteristics. It is the combination of the terms *organized* and *response* that is the key. Here organized means thoughtful, while response means action. There is a level of "thinking and acting" on purpose here (survival), low level though it may be. Thinking and acting on purpose is the key to ultimate unity, shalom, in this world. We can learn from this bacterial thinking and acting about our own thinking and acting.

Using the word thinking with microbes can cause problems for people. Many claim that this bacterial activity is simply a Pavlovian, conditioned, preprogrammed response, more like a reflex than a choice. I believe that it is more than that. There is actual wisdom in this response. They are responding to an environment in a way that can best be described as with cunning. In the case of tooth decay you do not need a brain to have brain-like communications in the biofilm. There is something deeper going on.

Schroeder quotes Freeman Dyson, "it appears that mind as manifested by the capacity to make choices is to some extent inherent in every atom."[46] He points out, "It explains how the energy of the creation, essentially light beams, could become alive and sentient and, able to feel love and joy and wonder. Divine wisdom was and is present, guiding and forming the way."[47] The secularist would disagree by stating that all of this came about by random chance. The big question is, "Does the development of the world from initial burst of energy through to the origin of sentient life seem random or guided?"[48] If it is random then there is no need for God. If it is guided, then we clearly need a guide—God. It is quite difficult to explain how consciousness can emerge from matter. It is also difficult to explain how a physical brain gives rise to the metaphysical mind. But it makes plenty of sense if things are the other way around—if mind is the source of matter. Since matter is built from energy, and energy is built from information, and information is a manifestation of wisdom, of the underlying metaphysical mind of our universe, then the metaphysical gives rise to our physical universe. In other words, the metaphysical God left some of his wisdom and his guidance in his creation when he withdrew.

Human wisdom is an advanced, higher animal type of this wisdom that God placed into the world. Its form is what we call our mind. Our mind is the metaphysical form corresponding with the physical brain. At the level of the mind, wisdom is engaged, integrating all of the brain functions, the mosaic of knowledge, reason and Faith thus empowering us to make conscious Level 3 responses to the challenges of our lives.

Using wisdom, Jim understands that all of his problems are related to each other. The economy affects his patients monetarily, which in turn affects their ability to buy his services. That affects his office, which affects his staff, their salaries, and their attitudes. Emotionally charged undertones can be present in the office. Patients pick up on those undertones and add their own problems to the mix. Jim also understands the problems at work can lead to problems at home and vice versa. At Level 3 Jim needs to use the mosaic of knowledge along with integrated wisdom to understand and solve these issues. He must use the science of dentistry to improve clinical results. At the same time, he must incorporate various dental practice management techniques to help solve issues related to staff, patient customer service, profitability, and his enjoyment of each day at work.

Kate at Level 3 is no longer a victim of cancer nor is she suffering from cancer. She is now fighting to cure her cancer. This fight is scientific and medical as well as religious, spiritual, and metaphysical. She will use any tool available in the mosaic of knowledge to help her win her fight. She will also integrate all the parts of her life, realizing that each part contributes to her as a whole individual. Kate is greater than the sum of her parts. In the new plan, her husband takes more care of the children, and they both work at home in a new Internet business. Her fight goes on.

As good as Level 3 responses sound, there remains one higher level. We move up to that level next.

Level 4 Response

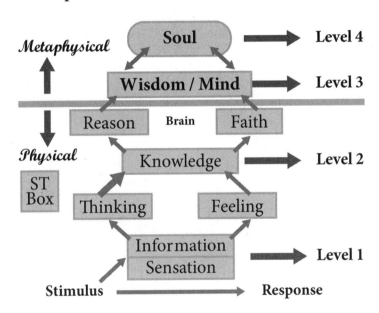

The source of a Level 4 response is the human soul. In the first chapter of Genesis, the Hebrew term "bara" occurs three times. It refers to the creation of something from nothing. There is no evolution involved because it is a characteristic endowed directly from God. We have already encountered bara in the Bible's first verse. There it is used in relationship to the creation of the entire universe—the Big Bang. As we just discussed in Level 3, at that point God created the universe with wisdom so that it could "evolve" without direct Divine intervention. Bara occurs a second time in reference to the soul of higher animals called Nefesh in Hebrew. This animal soul is a higher level of consciousness than universal wisdom-mind alone. It is an awareness concerning pleasure and pain.

The human soul, called the Neshamah in the Hebrew bible, is the third occurrence of the word bara. It can be defined as the conscience. Your human soul resides within your mind, which is your consciousness. The Neshamah is a special direct divine gift that, when you listen to it, helps you understand the unity of the world. It's not just that there is one God. It is that there is an oneness to everything, ShaLom. Your soul can help you find meaning and purpose. The Neshamah empowers you to have a connection to and conception of the metaphysical. That can only happen in something that is itself metaphysical. While mind and soul are both metaphysical entities, the mind is not the soul. The soul resides in the mind.

The soul, when faced with a stimulus and your proposed response, asks and helps answer the questions:

* Will this choice actualize my purpose?
* Will this choice increase my happiness (joy and inner peace)?
* Will this choice increase my sense of unity?

- ✦ Will this choice improve my connection with the Power and Loving Greater Than Ourselves?
- ✦ Will this choice increase my Holiness?
- ✦ Will this choice increase my soulfulness?

The human thus has:

- ✦ A physical brain
- ✦ A spiritual mind, wisdom (consciousness)
- ✦ An Animal soul (pleasure pain awareness-nefesh) &
- ✦ Human soul (moral conscience -Neshamah).

The animal drives (pleasure pain) are often in conflict with the human soul. The animal drives only know about family and self, but not about universal unity. It requires a human soul to be aware of the unity that is present in the universe.

Did human beings evolve from animals or did God create human beings? I answer yes to both of these questions.

The key is not that we evolved *from* animals but that we must evolve *beyond* animals.

Mere survival is possible through evolution alone. Meaningful survival, human survival, and the actualization of our human potential to do something of value and purpose require a spiritual evolution beyond nature alone. Human life is not simply about survival. The purpose of human life is **to survive "So That___!"** And you fill in that blank with your purpose, with your meaning and with your values.

We have evolved physically So That we can evolve spiritually!

Spiritual evolution begins with awareness of your conscience (human soul) inside your consciousness (mind - wisdom). The gift of the awareness of the infinite and of good and evil empowers you to be able to connect your parts to that whole. Then, using the mosaic of knowledge, you can gain the ability to find purpose and meaning overcoming challenges and solving problems in this physical world along *Your Path to Happiness.*

In this conscious search for conscience, and our attempt to connect to the unity of Infinity, the classic line of Judaism applies (Deuteronomy, 6:4):

"Listen Israel, the Lord is our God, the Lord is one."

This concept of unity, of one consciousness, is found in much of the world's wisdom literature:

* Hindus refer to it as the Atman.
* The Koran asserts the existence of a single absolute truth that transcends the world. The doctrine of the oneness of God in Islam is called Tawhid.
* The Oneness of God is one of the core teachings of the Bahai faith. Bahais believe that, although people have different concepts of God and his nature, and call him by different names, everyone is speaking of the same entity.
* Sikhs believe in one timeless, omnipresent, supreme creator. The opening verse of the Guru Granth Sahib

known as the Mool Mantra signifies this: *"There is only One God. The Name Is Truth. Creative Being Personified. No Fear. No Hatred. Image Of The Timeless One, Beyond Birth, Self-Existent. By Guru's Grace"*[49]

The key point here is that there is an all embracing wisdom that fills the universe. Everything (every-*thing*) is a manifestation of that eternal unity—a consciousness which many label as a God. When you touch that unity, you perceive and also experience a wonder within which you and all the rest of creation are embedded. You have reached a level of joyful inner peace, shalom, or happiness.

Jim has reached Level 4. This is the level of soulful decision making and the level of operating on purpose. Jim understands his purpose is to serve people using his knowledge, talents, and abilities as a dentist. This purpose comes from deep inside him—inside his soul. Looking at his life as an opportunity to fulfill that purpose empowers him to change the whole way that he looks at all of his problems.

Each problem is a challenge. Each problem is an opportunity to fulfill his purpose, to serve others. There is the challenge of a bad economy. The solution is to develop a more liberal financial arrangement policy along with increased treatment choices. There is a second economic challenge. The economy also affects his patients emotionally. Many would like to do treatments that they can no longer afford and are embarrassed by this situation. Many ask questions that they would not ask in other situations. Jim is beginning to realize that often patients are not angry directly at him, but instead they are angry at the situation that has developed in their lives. It turns out that Mrs. Collins is not angry at Jim. She is angry at Mr. Collins who is no longer working.

Actively listening to his patients is a way for Jim to connect to their problems through their souls. Applying the same active listening principles to his team, he can identify, understand, and begin to solve many problems with the help of the whole team. Jim is using his soul, his conscience, to make better decisions at work and at home. These Level 4 responses are leading Jim to much more joy and inner peace-happiness.

Kate at Level 4 has been healed from cancer and understands how to live with cancer. She may or may not ever be cured. She understands that, for her, cancer was a messenger for her family to change the way they were thinking and acting. They were not thinking as a family, but as individuals. They were acting in ways that were not supportive of each other. Cancer forced the family to deal with the problems. By consciously using conscience (soul), the family focused on the goal of healing each other. The family was able to work together to help Kate heal.

Kate became a model for the family itself. She modeled love, courage, strength, and Faith. Amazingly, the family was actually happier during this experience than they were before. The power of purpose overrides the pain of problems. Love overrode cancer.

So you go from a reflex with no processing (Level 1), with not much space between stimulus and response. By pausing you create a bigger space between stimulus and response in which you can think and feel and gain knowledge by processing information. Decisions made based on knowledge (Level 2) are better than those made on pure reflex. Pausing again between stimulus and response allows you to engage the mosaic of knowledge, use reason and Faith and reach a metaphysical, conscious level, that of wisdom using your mind (Level 3). However, the very best level to make decisions is at the level of the soul (Level 4). To make soulful decisions you must learn to listen to your soul. Your soul is the small still voice that will help guide you if you listen. It's your conscience speaking to you. Integrated with all other levels it becomes the best level at which to make decisions.

So when my father asks me, "How do you know?" my answer is, "imperfectly, climbing The Ladder of Learning using all the tools of knowledge and wisdom available to me."

Because God has withdrawn, we live in a world of paradox, uncertainty, and pluralism. How do we know if there really is a spiritual realm? How do we know if we humans really do have a unique soul? We never know for sure! We do not get absolute truth—God's truth. Instead we get human, imperfect, practical, partial truths—a mosaic of truth. We get actualities not reality. Under those conditions do we choose to focus on pain and problems, or upon freedom? Do we choose to take responsibility or do we blame? Will we learn to think and act on purpose? The test is ours, the choice is ours, and the responsibility is ours. We must learn to see both sides of any paradox as potentially being true, with both parts eventually emerging as a whole. We must value all legitimate paths to truth as described on The Ladder of Learning.

Listening To the Voice

Whenever my father and I engage in a discussion of religion, at some point my father asks his question, how do you know, but adds something special. For example, if we are talking about the Jewish Sabbath, my father would ask, "How do you know? Did God tell you?" My answer is usually, "Yes!"

What do I mean when I say God told me? We Jews have been listening to God for a very long time. In fact, about 4000 years ago Abraham became the first Jew by listening to God's voice.

I bring to you Abraham's story of hearing the voice, of listening through his soul. I bring it here because of the powerful messages it brings to our search for truth and doing the right thing. You do not have to be Jewish to appreciate the messages. You can be nonreligious or an atheist and still learn from the stories. If nothing else, you can learn more about what a 4000 year old religion, Judaism, has to say. Remember, I am only a messenger, and you do not have to agree with my message.

Before we get into the story itself, I would like to address one major complaint that people have against religion. It seems that each religion claims that it, and only it, has the truth. To be saved, you must follow us and only us. I am an observant Jew. Most of you would expect me to state that Judaism and only Judaism is true. I am sorry to disappoint you, but while Judaism believes in one God it does not believe in one exclusive path to salvation. We value differences. Unity does not mean uniformity. We can only achieve Harmony if there are differences, including differences in Faith. You don't have to be a Jewish person to be a man or woman of God. The righteous of every Faith, every nation, have a share in the world to come.

Abraham's story:

> *"And God said to Abram, go for yourself from your country and from your birthplace and from the house of your father, to the land which I shall show you. And I will make you a great nation and I will bless you, and I will make your name great, and you will become a blessing. And I will bless them that bless you and who curses you will I curse, and through you all the families of the earth shall be blessed. So Abram went as God had told him to."* (Genesis 12, 1-4)

Abraham heard a voice, "Go for yourself!" Leave your land, leave home, and leave your parents. Go for yourself. Go with your own family. Go to yourself. You are unique you are special. You have the potential to be a hero. You can take the hero's journey. You have a mission, a journey, a path to take. Discover your path. Discover your story. Go along your path and live your story. You are to begin your quest without knowing where it will take you ("to the land in which I shall show you"). Trust this voice. Go with God." End of the first sentence, end of the first stage.

Second sentence, second stage: Out of your relationship with God and with your family create a people, a nation, who will be faithful to God. God will bless you. A blessing is actually a granting of power and ability. It is not a granting of a result or a reward. It is a granting of potential. What one does with that potential is the key. Abram and his children are given potential for greatness. However, they must choose to actualize it through their thinking and acting. They can choose to become a blessing. Trust the voice, become a blessing.

Third sentence, third stage: Whereas I blessed you, so shall you be a blessing to those who will bless you, who connect to me through your example. Your children are to dedicate themselves to the Divine purpose of bringing happiness to the world by empowering others to do acts of service and love. In performing acts of service and love themselves, your children shall be role models for the other nations. Trust the voice, empower others.

Abram trusted the voice. He heard it in his soul. Abram went. We are all better off for that.

If we listen closely, we can all hear that voice even in this age of materialism, science, and philosophy. We can connect with the Power and Loving Greater Than Ourselves. Not only is this universe the result of a power beyond us, but that power lovingly brought us into being. That power listens to our prayers, cares about us, and has created for each of us a unique purpose and meaning. It is our responsibility to listen to the voice, find that purpose and meaning, and act upon it accordingly.

Like Abram, each of us walks down the path of life. We choose our way. Whatever path you choose, go on purpose.

Life is a journey. It is not a destination. As long as we are alive we never fully arrive. As long as we are alive, we are always in the process of walking down that path. Go for happiness. We must trust our inner knowing, our inner selves, and our soul. We must trust our metaphysical connection to the Power Greater Than Ourselves. That higher knowing is a true guide for our journey.

What about my journey? What I originally thought to be my journey, that of a dentist, has become something quite different. Dentistry has been wonderful for me. For 25 years I loved it. While it was my earlier journey, it was not my ultimate journey. My new journey has as its purpose empowering happiness—shalom. I do that by helping people to overcome challenges and achieve happiness using the healing power of values. Speaking and writing are how I actualize that why.

I am now traveling down a path of speaking and writing and changing people's lives in ways I never imagined possible. I have been gifted and blessed with special information from my experiences, and now I pass this on to you. Those experiences—a major bicycle accident, clinical depression, and Parkinson's disease—have made for a difficult and painful path. However, I still feel blessed.

Remember a blessing is a granting of power and ability. What you do with that potential is the key. It is a gift from God. While most of us think of a blessing as wholly positive, some call suffering a blessing in disguise. My bicycle accident and my Parkinson's disease are blessings in disguise. Any event or experience can be a blessing—a potential moment of spiritual growth. As we've discovered from the lessons of learning, you have the freedom to choose responsibility and purpose. Go up The Ladder of Learning thereby choosing to win and learn. Using the whole-parts-whole universal process and your path to happiness, we come to the understanding that this universe did not come into existence accidentally. Our lives are not without meaning. The universe exists and we exist because the Power and Loving Greater Than Ourselves, the one God, creator of all, brought us into this existence with his power, love, and wisdom. He brought each of us into existence on purpose for a unique purpose. We are here "So That___!" It is this belief more than any other that is a blessing giving us the potential for happiness, even in the presence of significant suffering pain and problems. The power of that purpose overrides the pain of problems. Our purpose empowers us to move from parts to whole, from Light to Love to Life and shaLom.

Why is Abraham chosen?

In an amazing passage we hear God's thoughts "For I know him (Abraham), that he will command his children and his household after him, and *they shall preserve the path of the Lord, to do what is right and just*; that the Lord may bring upon Abraham that which he has spoken of him." (Genesis 18:19)

Clearly Abraham was already a monotheist. His belief in the one Power Greater Than Ourselves enabled him to hear the voice that told him to go. His belief in that voice, in the mission and path upon which he embarked, emerged from and demonstrated his deep faith. From this passage however, it is clear that Abraham was chosen for a deeper reason. Abraham believed that this voice came from a God who was ethical.

Abraham's path was the path of searching for truth and doing the right thing. He did acts of loving service. We are told that this path is the path of the Lord—what I call *Your Path to Happiness*. Most important, however, is that he worked to pass the message contained in the voice on to his children and then to his household after him. Passing on the path of God to future generations comes from giving voice to the voice—by telling the story. Eventually the story comes to me.

So my first answer to my father's question, "How do you know, did God tell you?" is, "Yes, He did! He told me indirectly through Abraham who heard His voice and passed it down through the generations until it reached me. Just as Abraham heard the voice in his soul and started a Jewish path, so too I have heard that same voice in my soul, and I do my part in the continuing journey of our people down the Jewish path."

Other people have their path, their answers to their particular troubling questions and issues. We humans were all created in the image of the one God. That Power and Loving Greater Than Ourselves is the source of absolute truth, values, meaning, and purpose. The powerful creator of the universe is also the source of love. Unlike the views of the theists, God not only creates—He relates. Either directly, or through his messengers, He calls to each of us with his voice.

As members of the human family we can all hear the voice if we learn to listen carefully. However, we are also members of particular families. Each one hears a different aspect of the voice. Each family, culture, or religion has its own story, its own memory, and its own particular identity. My family, my father himself, has a particular story.

That story leads to my second answer to the question, "How do you know? Did God tell you?" My deeper answer to my father is, "I know because your story, which is also my story, is the story of a miracle. The fact that I am here to write down these words is itself a miracle." My father was born in Warsaw, Poland in 1930. His father, my grandfather, had one brother. My great-grandfather passed away in 1935. He was survived by twin brothers, Sam and Joe. Sam and Joe lived in the United States and were able to help 50 to 60 family members get out of Europe before the Holocaust. Sam was in Europe in 1936 and was God's messenger for my grandfather that he had better get out of Europe soon. It was very difficult to get out. It required a sense of purpose and a willingness to persevere in the presence of bureaucratic roadblocks. At any point my grandfather could've said, "This is just too hard. Perhaps all this talk of danger is just baseless rumors. Things aren't so bad here. I will just be optimistic and everything will turn out just fine. Forget the whole idea. I am staying right here." Thankfully, he listened to the voice inside that said, "Go for yourself."

In April of 1938, he received his visa. In May of 1938, my grandfather, grandmother, uncle, and father left Europe for the United States. Hitler invaded Poland in September of

1939. I am here writing these words because my grandfather listened to the voice and stayed on purpose. My family's survival is a miracle. I thank God for the blessing of life every single day.

Sadly, my grandfather's brother did not hear Sam's message as did my grandfather. He took his time. He did not believe fully in the message because he did not hear the voice. He did try, but in life trying is not enough. His date of departure was scheduled for early September 1939. That was not early enough. Hitler invaded on September 1, 1939. My grandfather's brother did not survive. He did not share my grandfather's level of purpose.

Think of how great a loss this was. Gone forever are several generations of individuals who could have passed on Abraham's story to humankind. Gone forever are several generations of individuals who could have filled the world with acts of loving service. Gone forever are several generations of individuals who could have transformed this world from ordinary to extraordinary. Gone forever are generations of individuals who could have actualized great purposes.

Purposeful thinking requires the use of every level of the Ladder of Learning. In particular, using the wisdom from mind and soul, from your conscious awareness that deep inside you is a small still voice of conscience, can help you find and stay on purpose. That purpose needs to guide your actions every day of your life. When you hear the message in your soul, and when you recognize that the messenger is the Power & Loving Greater Than Ourselves, you must do more than simply listen. You must act. You must act immediately. He who hesitates is lost. My grandfather's brother hesitated and he lost big-time!

We thus finish the section of the book with its focus on thinking on purpose by emphasizing that thinking must be followed up with action. Acting on purpose will be our focus in the next section.

So when my father asks me his question, "How do you know? Did God tell you?" I answer him, "Yes, He did. God speaks to me through your story, the miracle of your survival. Your survival became my existence and your story leads into my story. Our family story is a miracle. Inside every story of miracle is the voice of God. One need only listen closely to hear it. So dad, you ask me "How do you know?" I answer you because you and God have told me so!"

Every day that you are alive is a miracle. It is a blessing. It is a granting of potential and an opportunity. It is up to you to actualize and to achieve your potential. Make each day count. Find your purpose. Climb The Ladder of Learning and find out how to achieve that purpose. Then go for it. Pay attention to the messengers. Listen to their message, understand the message and then act on the message.

Through acts of service and acts of love each day you can

make a difference. That's what life is all about. We now turn to the second part of the book where we will focus on how to act on the message—acting on purpose.

Path Principles

* The Ladder of Learning empowers us to be able to learn any time that we lose.

* Stephen Covey says that there is a space between stimulus and response. The key to our growth and our happiness is how we use that space.

* You must use your knowledge to manage your feelings. Feelings can be used to empower us with the emotion, energy, and desire to act on our knowledge.

* Level 1 is the level of no choice. You respond to a stimulus with a reflex.

* Knowledge is an organized body of information. It is the result of investigating, studying, processing, and organizing information and sensation.

* Scientific Actualities are interim conceptions of objects defined by scientists using the scientific method.

* While science tells us *how*, religion tells us *why*.

* Science focuses on *what*, religion focuses on *what for*.

* Science is descriptive, describing our acts, whereas religion is prescriptive, telling us how we ought to act.

* "You think because you understand *one* you must understand *two*, because one and one makes two. But you must also understand ***and***."

* Understanding paradoxes leads to wisdom and better

decision-making.

* *Wisdom is integrated, balanced, and harmonious understanding.*

* Wisdom integrates physical and metaphysical understanding.

* Wisdom is taking proper, meaningful, and purposeful action.

* Wisdom is choosing appropriate values and acting on those values.

* With wisdom God created the heavens and the earth.

* The Neshamah is a special direct divine gift that, when you listen to it, helps you understand the unity of the world.

* The key is not that we evolved *from* animals, but that we must evolve *beyond* animals.

* There is an all embracing wisdom that fills the universe. When you touch that unity you perceive and also experience a wonder within which you and all the rest of creation are embedded.

* Listen to the Voice.

* This leads you to joyful inner peace, happiness—shalom.

The Ladder of Learning

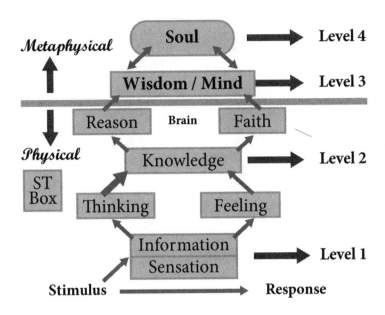

Part Two

Acting On Purpose

— CHAPTER 6: —

SEARCH FOR LIGHT:

FINDING YOUR PURPOSE AT

WORK AND AT HOME

Path prescription #6: The Timeless Values Connection

Paradoxically, this, the first chapter of the section of the book entitled *acting* on purpose, is focused on *thinking*. It involves thinking about our purpose at work and at home, which is a very active process of thinking. You must actively connect to the spiritual light from the Power and Loving Greater Than Ourselves. Using that connection, *The Timeless Values Connection,* you will search for your unique purpose here on earth.

Light is the first healing value and is the first step of *Your Path to Happiness.* Using the four healing values of Light, Love, Life, & ShaLom, the path to happiness HEALS us as it:

Helps
Empower
Acts of
Loving
Service

To be healed and to achieve happiness, we must first search for Help along our path. We must search for light, which helps to enlighten us about the sources of and solutions to our pain and problems. Light Empowers us to connect with our purpose and we then shine light on some darkened aspect of this world. We were created to help solve our own or someone else's problems by doing Acts of Loving Service. Once we understand our purpose and are connected to the light of that love, then each of us can actualize the unique contribution for which we were put here on Earth. By lighting a path for others and by healing others, we heal ourselves. Light is the first healing value.

When I began working on this chapter, I was in Dallas, Texas. Usually my wife works out of the Chicago office, but during the winter she works from a satellite office in Dallas. Most of this book was written in our suite in Dallas over the course of those months. This meant I had limited access to my sources. In particular, I wanted to use my grandfather's sermon on Light (my grandfather was a pulpit Rabbi) as a source for this section on Light. I did have a copy in my office at home but not with me in Dallas. I decided to try the Internet and to my surprise when I googled "Rabbi Paul Bender + Light," the following listing appeared on the third page.

LIFE'S HOLY *LIGHT*

File Format: PDF/Adobe Acrobat - Quick View *RABBI PAUL J. BENDER*. Duluth, Minnesota. Text: "*Light* is sown for the righteous, and joy for the upright in Heart." The Synagogue is filled to overflowing!... www.hebrewbooks.org/pagefeed/hebrewbooks_org_12791_31.pdf

I clicked on the hyperlink and there before me, on page 32 of the 1944 Rabbinical Council of America Book of Sermons, was my grandfather's sermon. The age of information is amazing. He gave this sermon more than 66 years ago on the holiest day of the Jewish year, the Day of Atonement, Yom Kippur, and here it was on the Internet.

While all of that impressed me, what I noticed next gave me goosebumps. The title of the sermon was "Life's Holy Light."[50] That is actually the essence of the title of my book, only backwards. As you will see in this chapter, being holy corresponds to doing acts of love. My grandfather's title is thus Life-Love-Light while my title is Light-Love-Life! As I read his sermon, it was as if I was listening to myself speak. Physically or metaphysically he had taught me this material.

He began, "The Synagogue is filled to overflowing! Israel is crowded into its place of worship, where once a year it gets its greatest strength through spiritual sustenance. Down through the corridors of time, our people have cast aside the ordinary to taste of something rare, of inspiration that flows through ethereal realms from God to man."

He continues pointing out that the service for the Day of Atonement begins with a recitation: "Light is sown for the righteous and joy for the upright of heart (Psalms 97:11)." What is the message of this passage on this night of the beginning of the Day of Atonement?

Before reviewing the message of the passage, he noted the importance of the opening lines uttered by any character in literature. The ultimate character can be found in the Holy Bible and that character is God himself. My grandfather notes:

> *"Nothing, I believe, could so vividly portray the God whom we worship as His opening words: "Let there be light." A God who made out of darkness light, is the God who took a meaningless void and created an intricate, meaningful universe out of this nothingness. A God who seeks out the souls of men and in their dark recesses infuses a never-ending light…a God who holds the promise of light and happiness to a world overcast with the darkness of "man's inhumanity to man"…is the God who created us in His image, and bade us follow His lead, and sow the seeds of light 'round about us among our fellow men.*

> *"If one spreads the light of Justice, he becomes a partner to God and His creation. If one brings the light of life to just one individual, he has established an entire world.*

The light of liberty, truth, and justice, is the goal of man═ and not in vain do men and women offer their lives for the restoration of these hallowed precepts. Our Torah in its entirety teaches the light of holy living through:

+ its precepts
+ in the daily tasks of mankind
+ in the Sabbath, the light of divine restoration of the soul
+ in keeping kosher, the light of restraint of animal instincts of the body
+ through hundreds of Commandments that have served as a guide to life here
+ through the teaching of kindness, aid, and succor to those less fortunate than we
+ through the light of knowledge to be gained through the study of God's own chosen word!

All those sacred principles are found as we turn the pages of the Book of Books, our Torah. Our ancestors lived such lives, and when the occasion demanded it, they died. Died? No, they live with us still! We, too, are bidden to live! We, too, are admonished to kindle and rekindle the everlasting flame of the light of life. And on this Holy Day of the beginning of the year, we are reminded indeed, 'Light is sown for the righteous, and joy for the upright in heart.'"

My grandfather has sent me a message. Through me, he has also sent you a message. What is that message?

It is a three-part message. First, God, the Power and Loving Greater Than Ourselves, is the source of **Light.** He is the source of healing values that bring solutions to our problems, meaning into our existence, and happiness into our lives. Light is the first healing value. While God hides that light, He plants that light as seeds. Spirituality is awareness of those seeds and of that light. We must use our Spirituality to find, feed, nurture, and grow those seeds of light, God's timeless values. Only then will we reap its rewards. I call this the Timeless Values Connection. *We must search for Light.*

Second, God wants us to plant seeds for others. Holiness is the process of bringing that spiritual light, those timeless values, into our daily productive life. Holiness is accomplished through holy acts, commandments (mitzvah in Hebrew). **A commandment, a mitzvah, is a quantum unit of holiness.** It is an act of responsible service, an act of love. It is a moment of connection with another. It is a moment of healing pain, of solving problems, or creating opportunities for others. *We must act with Love.*

The third and final message is that God's light, His values and sacred principles, can all be found in the Bible. In particular, the first five books of the Bible known to Jews as the Torah, contains the word God gave to Moses. The Torah contains Abraham's story, as well as ultimate timeless values, and its teachings have been passed down through the generations. We must rekindle the flame of that light of life in every generation. We must sow new seeds of light for the future generations. *We must create a holy Life & seek ShaLom—happiness.*

My grandfather's message to me is identical to my message to you. *Your Path to Happiness* involves using the four healing values of Light, Love, Life, & ShaLom! First we must search for God's metaphysical Light. That is the source of healing values, of our reason for being happy, and of our purpose. One can find that light anytime, but it shines brighter for Jews on Yom Kippur—a day of metaphysical light.

Yom Kippur is a 25 hour fast beginning from just before sunset and extending until after sunset the next evening. No food or drink is consumed. Most Jewish fast days commemorate some sad event in Jewish history. We have plenty of fast days. Yom Kippur is an exception to this. It is what I call a positive fast. On this one day every year we separate from the physical universe and from physical activities to focus on spirituality— on the metaphysical. The rest of the year we focus on this world, our physical space-time box, trying to make it a better place. But one day each year we separate from the physical ST box and attempt to make a special timeless values connection. We journey to a place beyond space and a moment beyond time. We connect to the metaphysical and remember our metaphysical purpose. I call that to **re-meta-member**, to remember the metaphysical, to remember God's timeless values. The Timeless Values Connection is thus re-meta-membering. After spending a full day re-meta-membering our values, our meaning, and our purpose, our souls are moved by the piercing sound from a ram's horn. At the finale, hearing that sound we re-meta-member our history, our values, and our purpose. Connecting with God's light, as we do on Yom Kippur, HEALS us. It **Helps Empower Acts of Loving Service** on our path to happiness for 365 more days.

You can find that light at any time. You can make your own Timeless Values Connection through your own re-meta-membering, through your own spirituality, and through your own particular religion. Spirituality is an awareness of that metaphysical memory. Holiness is re-meta-membering and then bringing that memory and those values into your daily activities, loving and serving others.

As you might recall from Chapter 3 in the whole-parts-whole process you are separated from God due to creation or your birth and you become one of the many parts. We want to be whole once again. It is that process of moving from parts back to wholeness that we defined as *Your Path to Happiness*. In the first step, Search for Light and the Timeless Values Connection, you connect to the timeless values contained in the metaphysical light. To connect using that process is to re-meta-member. That's what the first step of *Your Path to Happiness* is all about. Reconnecting with and remembering the metaphysical. Yom Kippur is the day we Jews reconnect with the metaphysical memory and re-meta-member. You can do this as well any time, and how to do this will be discussed later in this chapter.

To be human is to be able to remember, but not simply remembering a fact or a date or a face. That would be simple remembering. What we can do is to re-meta-member, which means to remember in a context, with meaning, and on purpose.

As I write this chapter, I am re-meta-membering my grandfather. My grandfather is no longer physically present. However, he lives on in my memory. In some ways that metaphysical memory is more real than physical reality. He becomes an actuality. Contained within that memory are stories of times we spent together.

I can re-experience being 12-years-old waiting and looking through the window at my home. It being Sunday morning, my grandfather was on his way to pick me up. I can remember how every Sunday morning we would drive together to his synagogue for morning prayers. I can still see him driving up to our house with a big smile and a big wave. I run out to the car get in, and off we go. I take in the familiar smell of his brand of cigar. Our conversation of course begins with his latest joke for me. We continue talking as we make several stops along the way. My favorite stop is for the bagels, lox, and cream cheese from the deli-bakery. That smell is a bit better than the cigars! At the synagogue I help him with the services in any way that I can. On this particular Sunday, I happen to be leading a part of the service. I look over at my grandfather, who, with a nod of his head and a secret smile in my direction, lets me know that I'm doing just fine. Little did I realize at the time that I would be the Cantor for Jewish High Holiday services for many years at several synagogues. It all started then. On the way back home we have a great conversation about God, free will, and what the Chicago White Sox will do in today's doubleheader. Here I am back home. What a great morning!

Within that memory my relationship with him continues today. As long as I continue to remember my experiences with my grandfather, he will be here right next to me. I re-meta-member and connect to his values, to his teachings, and to his purpose, all of which are metaphysical characteristics. I bring my grandfather back and reconnect to him, his life, and the messages that he has always had for me, and in this way his story lives on. My grandfather lives once again through me whenever I re-meta-member and bring him back.

Just as I can re-meta-member my grandfather, I can also re-meta-member the Power and Loving Greater Than Ourselves. I can make a Timeless Values Connection to that power and loving and bring that power and loving back into my physical life in the ST box. I can connect to the hidden face of God and bring him back.

To re-meta-member is to bring the past into our present consciousness. We were not physically present at historical events and we are no longer present in our own past events.

To remember is a metaphysical activity. Not only do we remember the facts, but we remember them in a context. This gives meaning and value to past events. Meaning that we create emerges from our memory. We recreate past moments using our metaphysical memory, and in so doing we re-meta-member. We can use that meaningful memory to help find our purpose. We can use our past, our story, our history to help us discover our identity, our future purpose, and create our future story. Creating and living that story brings us shalom—happiness. That metaphysical connection is The Timeless Values Connection.

The Timeless Values Connection

What does it mean to make a timeless values connection? We connect to the metaphysical light and to the higher values found in the metaphysical dimension. There we connect with God's holy, timeless values. Using those values, we search for our primary healing value, our purpose. We will return to the space time box and act on that value, that purpose.

The Timeless Values Connection is perhaps best exemplified by the story of Jacob's ladder (Genesis 28:10-22).

> *"Jacob was fleeing from his brother. At nightfall he went to sleep and dreamed of a ladder with its base on the Earth and its top reaching into heaven. He saw angels going up and down the ladder. At the top of the ladder Jacob saw God. God told Jacob he was to be the one*

who would pass on the story of Abraham. When Jacob awoke he said, "God is in this place and I, I did not know. How awesome is this place! This is none other than the house of God, and this is the gate of heaven."

While there are many ways to read this story, I believe it is a search for purpose and meaning. It is *Your Path to Happiness.* Jacob could be asking the question "Why me?" as he flees from the danger his brother posed. We have learned that this question is really a question of why do I suffer, why do I exist, and what is my job here on Earth. To find answers to these questions Jacob becomes "an angel," a messenger with a message from Jacob to God—"Why me?" Up he climbs toward God, into the metaphysical realm at top of the ladder. There, listening to God, he hears the voice. The voice answers his question by revealing his purpose. As an angel, now a messenger from God, on purpose, he descends the ladder. Upon awakening, he realizes what an incredible experience he's just had. Notice his first sentence, especially the doubling of the word "I." God is in this place, and I had no idea that that was true. This place is a gate to heaven. Any place can be a gate to the dimension of timeless values. We need spirituality, an awareness that such a place exists. Any place can be such a place I now know what earlier "I, I did not know." **I now know the "Why me?" the "I" that I did not know.** In connecting with God and his values, I now know more about my purpose and my values. In connecting to the "Thou" I know more about the "I." I have seen His Light and

I see the world in a different Light. I return to my life in this world with a light shining from inside me, radiating joy. I am happy from the inside out. I'm on my path to happiness.

Jacob's Ladder is not only a metaphor relating to The Timeless Values Connection. It relates to the Ladder of Learning in our previous chapter as well as *Your Path to Happiness* as discussed in Chapter 3. In each of these cases there is a ladder that starts in the physical and leads into the metaphysical. Something is discovered in that metaphysical realm and its lesson is then brought back from the metaphysical into the physical. In the physical world, in our space-time box, in this place, God is present yet I did not know it. God is hidden in the physical world. Our job is reconnecting with God by climbing Jacob's ladder and connecting to God in the metaphysical realm and "bringing him back" by bringing his timeless values into our daily lives.

You do not need Yom Kippur or any special place to make The Timeless Values Connection. Meditation, prayer, spiritual reading, a walk in nature, listening to spiritual music, or any of a number of spiritual practices can help you climb the ladder to make The Timeless Values Connection.

To gain a better understanding of The Timeless Values Connection we will use the values from the lessons of learning from Chapter 2. Those values are Freedom, Responsibility, and Purpose. When we match those three values with The

Timeless Values Connection, the result is:

Timeless = Freedom
Values = Responsibility
Connection = Purpose

Let's investigate this more fully.

Timeless = Freedom

What is time? Think about it. This is a very hard question to answer. Let's approach it from the beginning of the book of Genesis. What is the first thing created? Once again, here's the first verse of the Bible:

"In the beginning God created the heaven and the earth."

We've already said that the first word in Hebrew, Breisheet, can mean "with wisdom" God created the universe. The second way of interpreting the word is "In the beginning of..." The question is in the beginning of what? The answer given by Rabbi Elijah of Vilna (18th-century) is: in the beginning of time. Notice the word "beginning" is a word involving time. The first creation was *time*! Why time? What is so important about time? We return to the question, "What is time?"

Time is a blessing from God empowering us with an arena for changing and becoming more than we are today.

Remember, we are human becomings. We become through time and we can change. Why is changing so important? **Our ability to change is the source of our freedom. We have free choice—we can choose to change because change is possible in this world.** We can *choose* to be happy. We can *choose* to become someone who achieves happiness. We can win or learn. When we say time HEALS all wounds we mean it **H**elps **E**mpower **A**cts of **L**oving **S**ervice. Time empowers purposeful thinking and acting, being of service to others. Serving others heals us.

God, the timeless, withdraws and thus creates time. We experience the flow of that time in our space-time box. Brian Green, professor of physics and mathematics at Columbia University, in his book *The Fabric of the Cosmos* notes that time is the bookkeeper of change. We can tell that time has passed by seeing that things "now" are different from how they were "then". Change has occurred. Time is what provides the potential for this change to be actualized. He paraphrases John Wheeler, who said, "Time is nature's way of keeping everything from happening all at once."[51] For God everything does happen all at once. God exists in the eternal present.

Gerald Schroeder tells a story in the book *The Science of God* addressing this issue. I have adapted it with his permission.[52] He prefaces his story by pointing out that we must take note of the fact that we are dealing with two frames of reference. Our frame of reference is inside the flow of time, while God's frame of reference is outside the flow of time. God, being outside of the space-time box experiences all time at once, is an eternal now.

To get a better understanding of this, imagine going out into the dark tonight and seeing a new bright star in the sky. What you're looking at is a distant star that exploded, forming a supernova, and its glow had just reached the Earth. Let's say it was located 170,000 light years from Earth. The light of that exploding star had started its journey through space 170,000 (Earth) years before you first saw it. For all that time the secret of the explosion was locked in its photons. At the moment of the explosion, if a Neanderthal hominid had gazed to the heavens, he would not have seen anything unusual. The light of the supernova was still 170,000 light years away. After another 150,000 years, Cro-Magnon man was making tools but if he looked up in the sky he would not see a supernova. Thirty-three hundred years ago Jews were crossing the desert on their way to the Promised Land. If one of them looked to the sky, the supernova would not have been visible. Neither would it have been visible about 2000 years ago as Paul of Tarsus walked along the road to Damascus. If Gutenberg had taken a moment off from working on his new printing press to go outside and look up into the sky, he would not have seen the supernova. If a soldier in World War II, while liberating a concentration camp in Europe, looked up into the sky, he would not have seen the supernova; and if you had gone out last night and looked into the sky, you would not have seen the supernova either. Only tonight, when the photons arrive at Earth, will the supernova finally be visible. By this time 170,000 years would have passed on Earth.

What if an imaginary you (minus all material aspects of yourself) traveled in a massless spaceship going at the speed of light and traveled next to the photons from the supernova for the 170,000 Earth years? How much time would this imaginary you have experienced? The amazing answer is zero. *No time would have passed!* As Einstein has taught us, the faster one travels relative to another object, the slower time flows for the traveler relative to the flow of time measured by the stationary observer. At the speed of light, time ceases to flow altogether. At the speed of light, everything that took place during the 170,000 years occurred simultaneously. You would experience past, present, and future as having blended into an eternal, ever present, unending now. You would experience Neanderthal and Cro-Magnon man, the crossing of the desert, Paul, Gutenberg, and the World War II soldier all at once. What does that mean? I have no idea. I have never been outside of time. However, this gives me some idea, limited as it might be, of God's view. Just as on the light beam no time passes, so too for God, as the eternal present, no time passes. God, existing outside of time, knows the ending at its beginning. Just as on the light beam, all of history occurs at once. God's knowing is quite different from our concept of knowing.

God's "experience" of time is quite different from ours. This is what preserves our freedom of will—our freedom of choice. Our freedom comes from our existence in time. God's freedom, however, is beyond time. God's freedom is timeless. His "knowing" outside of time does not affect our "knowing" inside of time. God says, "I will be what I will be." (Exodus 3:14) In other words, I have freedom outside of time. I grant you freedom within time.

Since God and his freedom exist outside of time, God and his values are timeless. God's timeless values are absolute truths. They are not part of this changing world of ours. They are permanent. Your freedom comes from existing within time, your arena for changing and your ability to become more than you are today. You have the freedom to choose to connect with timeless values and your purpose found in the metaphysical realm. You can then actualize those values and purpose in the space-time box over time. Climbing the Ladder of Learning and human change requires time. Time is your arena for changing—for the freedom to choose your future on purpose. You can choose to ignore that freedom and become a victim or take advantage of that freedom and journey on purpose along your path to happiness thereby becoming a victor. It's your choice. Will you choose to connect to darkness and entropy or will you choose to connect to light, spirituality, and Holiness? In short will you connect to your purpose? It's your choice.

Values = Responsibility

Living within time and experiencing past, present, and future gives us freedom of choice. The questions then become:

- On what basis do we make our choices?
- How are we to make better choices?
- What is our responsibility?

We must learn how to make choices on purpose and we must connect with our purpose. The question arises once again: How do you know? You know through Timeless Values.

Value is:

1. The relative worth, merit, importance, or usefulness of something.
2. The worth of something in terms of exchange.
3. The significance or importance of something.
4. An ideal accepted by some individual or group.

Each of us has a set of values, which represent our belief system and which come from many sources. They come from the way we were raised as children, from the experiences we've had, from our talents, interests, and our unique personalities. Values also come from the society in which we live and the religion in which we participate, as well as from influential individuals in our lives. The question is, though, "Are your values timeless values?" The more your personal values align with timeless values, the higher will be your levels of inner peace and happiness.

We must connect to God's light, which is a conduit to timeless values. God and his truths exist outside of the flow of time and outside of space. Light is a conduit into that timeless realm. We can "hitch a ride on the light beam" and go on a journey and a quest in search of timeless truth and values. Once we connect with those timeless values, internalize them, take them into our souls, (that is into our conscience), we must then return to the ST box and return into the flow of time. Then, empowered with timeless values, we can make better choices. Making better choices puts you on *Your Path to Happiness.*

Hyrum Smith in his book, *The 10 Natural Laws of Successful Time and Life Management,* discusses the importance of values in our search for happiness. Happiness comes from "inner peace, which is the transcendent feeling of fulfillment and well-being that we all seek…The secret to achieving inner peace lies in understanding our inner core values…and then seeing that they are reflected in the daily events of our lives. In other words, doing a better job of managing your time is meaningless unless you are managing it to accomplish those things that are of greatest importance in our lives."[53]

Our core values are those things in our lives that are most important to us. Here we must emphasize the important over the urgent. The urgent seems to be important, but often it is not. Happiness is the process of accomplishing those things in our lives that are most important to us. It is not a process of accomplishing those things that are most urgent to us. A ringing phone can be urgent, yet not important. An evening with your child may not seem urgent (after all there is tomorrow night), but it is certainly important. Important things rarely seem urgent unless we make them urgent. We often place the urgent before the important. The key is to make sure that your daily activities reflect your deepest core values. That is your responsibility.

As you learned in Lesson 2, responsibility is your ability to respond to any condition in alignment with your core values, which should be timeless values. It is your response to your God-given abilities and means taking control of your life. You control your life by controlling your time, and this means controlling the events of your life through your choices. You must learn to understand which events you can control and which ones you cannot control, and then control those events that matter most.

Therefore, you must answer two questions: First, what are the highest values, the greatest priorities, in your life? Second, of these values, which of them is most important to you? So, you need to identify your values and rank them in order of importance. You can respond to any event based on what value that event reflects and its ranking. This is especially helpful when two significant values collide. It will be of tremendous value to you if you think this through in advance and prioritize a list. Although the decision may be difficult, even painful, you will most likely have a level of inner peace knowing you chose your highest priority.

The following is an example of prioritizing values. Take four common values: things, people, principles (universal principles upon which moral societies are built, what we have been calling timeless values, _not_ personal values), and money. How would you rank them from highest to lowest (1-4) value? Notice that any one of these values could be ranked anywhere from 1-4. What would be best? Let's take them two at a time. What is more important:things or people? For most of us the answer is an easy one:people. Relationships in our lives are more important than the things we have. If we violate that value judgment, we can end up with poor relationships and very little happiness.

Let's look at the next two. What is more important: universal principles (timeless values) or money? Although few of us would have a problem ranking these values, many of us have trouble living according to that ranking. Clearly, principles are a higher value than money.

Thus far we have two groups. Group 1 contains the winners: people and timeless values. Group 2 contains the losers: things and money. Starting with group 2, which has a higher value: things or money? Here is where purpose begins to enter the picture. To decide which one has a higher value, you need to know the purpose of each one. If your purpose is to have one or two items that do not cost much and you don't care about anything else, you could choose things over money. However, if your purpose is to become financially independent, you must learn to value money over things. When faced with the choice between putting aside money into your long term investment plan and buying some "thing", success requires valuing money over things. Obviously, if one of those things is food, clothing, or shelter, you put your long term plan on the back burner for a while.

Now let's look at group 1. Which has a higher value: people or universal principles (timeless values)? To save us a chapter long conversation (during which, only I would get to speak) let me just say this. Much as we must value people, we must value universal principles first. Timeless values, ultimate principles, are the objective source of how we can judge our own individual values and know how to rank them. They come from a Power & Loving _Greater_ Than Ourselves; the source of truth, of right and wrong, of eternal ethical and moral standards, and of timeless values by which we can judge our actions as well as those of others. Remember the words of Rabbi Lawrence Kushner back in Chapter 2 "The first commandment is: I'm God. The second commandment is: You're not!" Putting people first turns people into God. Having appropriate relations with other people requires understanding the principles of relationships to the best of our abilities (to be perfectly human is to know imperfectly), as well as valuing the use of those principles. Thus, principles are a higher value than people.

The final result of our ranking of these four values is:

Principles

People

Money

Things

Having such a prioritized list of values HEALS us. It **Helps Empower Acts of Loving Service** that are most important to us. When your activities each day are based on your core values, you have joy and inner peace. You experience a sense of balance, harmony, and wholeness that can heal you from problems, pain, and suffering.

As previously stated, your primary healing value, your purpose, emerges when you evaluate and rank your values. In the last section of this chapter I will help you identify and rank your values. We will identify your USP—your unique and special purpose. We will identify what added value you bring into this world.

Connection = Purpose

We began our search for purpose by asking the question "Why me?" In the introduction we broke this into three questions:

1. Why do I suffer from pain and problems? What is the purpose of pain and problems?
2. Why do I exist? What is my purpose and what value am I to add to the universe?

3. Why am I in business? What is the purpose and

meaning of my work?

The answers to these questions are found by connecting to timeless values. How do we do that? We separate from the material world (ST box) and connect with the Light of the metaphysical world (re-meta-membering). Jonathan Sacks notes, "Memory is my story…Memory is about identity… We are the story we tell about ourselves. History answers the question, 'What happened?' Memory answers the question, 'Who am I?'"[54]

When searching for meaning and purpose in life, story is more powerful than philosophy. Rabbi Sacks refers to the work of Jerome Bruner[55] in saying that philosophy (and science) attempt to explain the particular as it fits into a universal structure (Plato's concept of knowledge and truth). It uses the general rule if X then Y. Story, on the other hand, focuses on the particular—a specific time in a specific space with specific people (the Sophist view of knowledge). It uses a different general rule: "Once upon a time X happened, and then Y."

In philosophy "then" signals inevitability, but in story, anything can happen. One cannot predict the human response to any stimulus. Story connects directly with our souls with no need to climb the ladder of learning. We love stories because we want to know what is going to happen and we can never be sure what that will be before the end of the story. Stories are thus closer to the human experience than philosophy.

An excellent example of this is the story of Job. In this biblical story a God fearing, moral, ethical, and basically wonderful person, Job, is put through significant unjust suffering. He loses all his children and possessions, and experiences significant physical pain. At the end of the story, God speaks to Job. Job is told that neither he nor any other human can understand the complex, intricate workings of God and his universe. What we seem to have here is a philosophical statement of Lesson 1. Absolute truth exists, but we will never know it absolutely. Uncertainty separates us from God's knowledge. We will never know for sure why we suffer. We would expect, with God having made his philosophical point, that the book would end here, but interestingly enough, there is a final chapter. Job gets a new family, rebuilds his wealth, and goes on with his life. This seems to detract from the philosophical point of the existence of suffering for no apparent reason.

Here we see story overriding philosophy. Job cannot bring back those who are dead. He cannot change history, but he can choose the next page of his history. He can write a new story. He can have a second family. Having that second family is not recreating his first family. It is being responsible and going on as best one can without blame, looking forward not backwards.

We are not free to choose our conditions, but we are entirely free to choose our response to those conditions. Job chose not to be a continual victim stuck in the past and crying about past outrages. Instead he focused on surviving and being a victor. He focused on what he could build from what he had left. As Yitzhak Perlman said, "our task is to make music with what remains." Job chose to make a new Timeless Values Connection and connect to what Light that remained to find new Love, to build a new family, to build a new Life, and to seek whatever level of happiness, ShaLom, he could achieve. He stayed on purpose and he HEALS—he Helps Empower Acts of Loving Service. He did not deny the pain of his lost family. He still had their memory, and through this memory and his story, their lives, their identities, their meaning, and their purpose live on. Story trumps philosophy.

Stories make us human. When we listen to stories they connect directly to our souls and they connect directly to the top rung of the Ladder of Learning, and Jacob's ladder. There is no need to climb up the ladder. If we listen beyond the silence we can hear the voice within. This is told in the story of the Prophet Elijah (II Kings: 18).

Elijah had become a political refugee running away from the king and queen of Israel. Alone, he ended up in the Sinai desert at Mount Sinai.

Now, at this point in the story we expect some serious special effects. After all, this is Elijah, the man of special effects, on the mountain of Sinai, the site of some of the greatest special effects in history. So here it comes—behold, the Lord passed by, and a great and strong wind rent the mountains and broke the rocks into pieces before the Lord. Wow, this is cool! This must be it—the moment of revelation. But wait…the Lord was *not* in the wind. After the wind, came an earthquake. Surely now we're going to get the revelation from God. This is a great special effect. But the Lord was *not* in the earthquake. After the earthquake a fire came. This has got to be it. But the Lord was not in the fire. Now pay attention to the amazing phenomenon that occurred next—"and after the fire came **a still small voice.**" When Elijah heard the still small voice he wrapped his face in his mantle and went out to the entrance of the cave. It was then that a voice came to him and he received his revelation.

This revelation is not from the outside. It is from the inside. It is a still small voice, which is a voice only heard by our souls. The soul in each of us is capable of hearing the Word of God and connecting to the Word of God. It is our Soul that gives us the connection, the ability to communicate, to have a relationship with the Power and Loving Greater Than Ourselves, and to make the Timeless Values Connection.

Rabbi Jonathan Sacks[56] points out that it's not difficult for the creator to make a home for humanity. What is difficult is for human beings to make room for God. The holy is a metaphysical area where heaven and earth meet. That meeting place is where God rules—not mankind. When God created the universe, he withdrew, leaving ordinary space time. We, by connecting to God and his values and by bringing those values into ordinary space-time, bring God back into that space and it becomes holy once again. The ordinary is a space that God makes for us, while Holiness is the space we make for God. Holiness is not just what we do, but also the kind of person we become.

The rabbi of Kotzk asked a number of learned men who were visiting him this question, "Where is the dwelling of God?" They laughed at him: "What a thing you ask! Is not the whole world full of God's glory?" Then he answered his question, "**God dwells wherever man lets him in.**" This is the ultimate purpose—to let God in. We can let him in only where we really stand, which is where we live the true life. If we connect with others in our time space box, through acts of service and acts of love, we can make the space-time box our dwelling and a dwelling for the Divine presence. God said (Exodus, 25:8), "Make for me a holy place through your acts of service, acts of love and I will dwell within you." God HEALS us. God Helps Empower Acts of Love and Service.

Discover Your Values and Your Purpose at Work and at Home

At this point in the chapter, I can imagine hearing you say, "Enough explanation. I'm still waiting for a practical way of finding my highest values and my purpose." Well then, let's get to it.

There are three goals that we have at this point. First, we want to have a prioritized list of values. Second, we want to understand the general purpose of human life. Third, we want to identify our unique personal purpose at work and at home.

Creating a Prioritized List of Values

Step 1: Collect all the things that you will need and have them together on your desk or in a place where you enjoy working. Many people enjoy doing this kind of activity outside in a place of natural beauty. The details of this process are up to you. You will need:

+ A pad of paper
+ Pens, markers, highlighters and pencils Or a computer to capture some of your thoughts as they occur.
+ Eight or Sixteen 3 x 5 index cards

Step 2: Use some relaxation, meditation, visualization, or prayer technique to make a timeless values connection. There are many books and texts on these techniques. In an upcoming workbook I plan on covering this in more detail.

Step 3: Do the following series of procedures while you are in the timeless values connection:

1. Ask yourself this question:What are my highest values?
2. Listen for answers—ultimate timeless values. Be patient, it may take quite a while.

3. Write down any value that comes to you, but do not judge it yet. The purpose is to first generate a very large list.

4. It is best to start with your own list. It is also fine to use lists written by others. I have listed many possible choices of values in the *Appendix*.

5. Once you have your list of all the values that you can think of, it is time to prioritize them.

6. Go through the list and highlight those values that immediately impress you as being important, but not urgent. Also highlight those values that you believe are timeless values. Do not spend too much time thinking about each one.

7. Make a new list of these highlighted items.

8. Repeat this procedure until you have 16 values on one page (for some people using eight values works out better. For demonstration purposes we will use eight).

9. Take the index cards and place one value on each card.

10. Now lineup all eight of the index cards up in one column as in Figure 1 (with 16 cards the concept is the same).

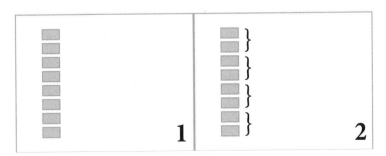

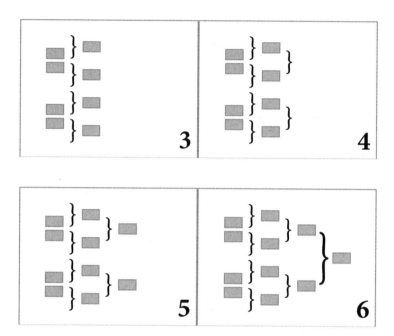

11. In your mind, place imaginary brackets around the first two cards as you would in a sports tournament. Repeat this all the way down for the full eight index cards yielding four brackets (the four brackets are shown in Figure 2).

12. Now have the two values cards "compete" against each other to determine which one is the "higher" value. This is a similar exercise to the one that was performed on page 230-232 with the example of prioritizing values. You choose. Take the "winner" and move it to the point of the bracket. Leave the other card where it is. Repeat this for all brackets as shown in Figure 3.

13. Repeat this as shown in figures 4, 5, and 6.

14. Here is a four-value example using the values listed on page 230:

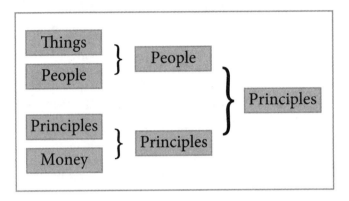

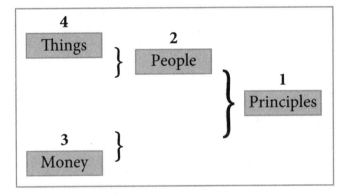

15. In theory, the card that wins the tournament should be your highest value and this is your primary healing value.

It does not always work out this way for a variety of reasons. However, it does get you much closer to a final result. By leaving all of the cards out as you go along, you can now begin to rearrange these cards in a more refined manner. Challenge the order that you have established. Subject each value to questions as to whether you would truly choose that value over the values that you have ranked lower. Re-meta-member times in your life where each of these values were tested. Think ahead into the future as to how you believe you should think and how you should act. You should be able to take the eight or 16 cards and put them in order of importance to you. You should now have a prioritized values list. The top card should be your primary healing value. It is also very likely to be your highest purpose, as well as your reason to be happy.

Step 4: Write a paragraph on the back of each card summarizing the importance of each value to you.

Step 5: Relax and return to the ST box with gratitude for the learning that you have achieved.

These cards should be read daily, reviewed deeply weekly and monthly, and revised annually. In the first few weeks you may want to revisit and revise them several times. Compare and contrast these values that you have come up with to those of your religious/spiritual background. Test for alignment and make adjustments as you deem necessary.

General Purpose

Our general purpose in life is to love, to serve, and to solve problems for each other. Purpose is the flipside of problems. If there were no problems we would have no purpose. Staying on purpose HEALS others. Purpose **H**elps **E**mpower **A**cts of **L**oving **S**ervice. Happiness is achieving the joyful actualization of your meaning and purpose.

Discovering Your Own Personal Purpose

Why do you exist? Your general purpose is to serve, to love, and to solve problems. You are here in this world "So That___!" Your responsibility in this business of life is to fill in that blank and discover a way of serving others that:

+ Aligns and connects with timeless values, soulfulness, and wisdom.
+ You find meaningful.
+ Others value.
+ Gives you joy.
+ You do well.

Why are you in business? Your business purpose is to solve particular problems for particular individuals. In other words, your business purpose is your USP. The letters USP usually stand for **U**nique **S**elling **P**roposition. It answers the question why should I buy from you as opposed to anybody else. I think a better focus is on solving problems. Therefore I use the term USP to represent the phrase "your Unique Solution to my Problem". It is the answer to three questions:

1. What is the problem that you solve?
2. What is your systematic solution to the problem?
3. What makes you unique and different from other businesses? (Why should I use you?)

In the history of the entire universe there has never been another you. You are special, unique, and of infinite worth. You must search for and find the answer to the question, "What added value were you put here to provide?" In other words, "What is your "So That___!"? You must discover how you can fill in that blank with a reason to jump out of bed every morning filled with the drive to achieve happiness in your life.

So, for what purpose am I here? What is my "So That___!"? Everyone has to fill in the blank differently. You must determine how to fill in that blank mostly by yourself and for yourself. Fill it with purpose and meaning, with something that drives you to exceed expectations, with something that creates a picture in your mind of a life well lived, with something that you will be proud to be known for. By acting on the answer, you can become extraordinary.

To find your "So That___!" you must listen to the messages of your messengers. Many of us do not even know that we have messengers, much less that these messengers carry significant messages. Do you see messengers in your life? Do you hear and understand and then live their messages? How do you know them? How do you hear them? How do you find your purpose? How do you find your "So That___!"?

To find your ST go back to Chapter 1 and review the two questionnaires included in that chapter. Whether you fill that out or not, take a copy of those questionnaires with you. Go off by yourself and try to use the Timeless Values Connection and listen. Review the old questionnaires and answer those questions. You may be surprised at the difference in your perspective since Chapter 1. Then ask yourself the following questions. Be sure to listen for a while for an answer.

1. What do you truly love to do? What gives you joy?

   _____

2. What do you love to do that helps or serves others?

   _____

3. What do you love to do that gives you meaning?

   _____

4. What are you good at? What do you naturally find easy and fun to do?

   _____

5. What is something that you do that while you are doing it time flies?

_____

6. What do you want to be remembered for?

_____

7. How would you like people to remember you?

_____

8. When people tell your story, what will that story be?

_____

9. Will your story be a comedy, a tragedy, a mystery, a romance, or will it be an epic where you are the hero and you do extraordinary things?

_____

10. What is the theme (purpose) of your story?

_____

Remember it is your choice. You have freedom. Not freedom from everything, but freedom to choose your story. When freedom is combined with responsibility, you have a chance to choose an excellent meaningful story—an extraordinary story. If you're doing something that has meaning to you, that gives you joy and that you do well, then you know you're on the right track. That doesn't mean it will not be hard, nor does it mean you won't have problems. Of course you will. But you can win or learn. One of the lessons you may learn could be the discovery that you are not yet doing what you were put here to do. That is probably one of the most important lessons that you will ever learn.

Although I loved doing dentistry, did an excellent job of it, and found it meaningful, the time had come to move on to a new mission. It was time to shift from the private practice of dentistry to speaking in dentistry and elsewhere. That was my shift. That is my story.

You must discover your story. You must discover the theme of your story and therefore the purpose of your life. I cannot find your purpose for you. I cannot tell you what your purpose is. No one can tell you your purpose except you. You must discover your own purpose.

You must listen to the messages of the messengers. You must stop, pause, close your eyes, and listen. Listen to the messengers giving you messages through the small, still voice inside you. Open your eyes, read scriptures, and Listen to the messages through Scripture. Listen to the messengers giving you messages through nature, other people, and even suffering. Only you can hear your messengers and only you can hear their messages.

Purpose Statement

A purpose statement is a single sentence summarizing your purpose. Many books have been written on this subject alone. It is a form of USP in that it represents your **U**nique and **S**pecial **P**urpose. This statement can be used to increase your focus and concentration and motivate you each day all day long.

As an example my purpose statement is: I exist So That I can serve by empowering ShaLom. Notice that the first part applies to everyone: "I exist So That I can serve by." On the other hand the last two words (in my case—empowering ShaLom) apply only to you or your business team. The last two words take the form of: _____a_____ing_____b_____; where a = a loving activity (a verb), while b = some object of the activity. You may find that your "a" and "b" are your first two values from your prioritized list of values. You will find that "b" items can be found in your values or the values listed in the first list in the *Appendix*. Some people find that they need other options for the verb ("a"). The *Appendix* has a second list, with verbs to help you choose your "a."

This is not the only way to formulate a purpose statement. For me another example is "I Empower ShaLom using the healing power of values." I could go on and on. For you the key is being creative and going through the process of crafting your purpose statement. Use it as the theme of your story, the life that you are creating each day.

Finding your purpose will not happen overnight. Unless it is time and you are truly ready, and you get a gift of the right messenger at the right time, you may be blessed with the perfect messenger at the perfect time, and you may have a chance to understand it right away. That's not the way it usually works. It is usually hard. There is no right way to find your purpose. Each of us is unique and each of us has a different purpose. Each of our strengths is different from that of others. Each of our paths toward our purpose is different. Each of us follows our **Unique** and **Special Path.**

Ask yourself these questions:
- Do I find tremendous joy in this activity?
- Do I do it well?
- Does it give me meaning?

One reason that it is so hard today to try to find your purpose is that it is so hard to find purpose through materialism. You cannot find purpose and deep meaning in a world that is simply physical. If there is no spiritual, there is no ultimate meaning. You can try to find meaning, you can make up your meaning, but ultimately there is no meaning.

You can become what you dream as long as it's in alignment with your talents, with what gives you joy, and what you find meaningful in this world. Connect to the Power and Loving Greater Than Ourselves. Make the Timeless Values Connection. Ask for a messenger, and listen for the message that the messenger brings. Only when you stop, pause, close your eyes, and listen can you discover that which you were meant and ought to become. Then it's up to you to make the extraordinary choice and become that vision of who you can be.

That vision can often be accomplished closer to home, closer to where you are today, than you might believe possible. Martin Buber in his book, *The Way of Man*, tells a story that Rabbi Bunam used to tell of a person of great property who never lost Faith in God. One night he dreamed that someone told him to look for a treasure in Prague, under the bridge leading to the King's Palace. When his dream recurred a third time, the man prepared for the journey and set out for Prague. But the bridge was guarded day and night, and he did not dare to start digging. Nevertheless he went to the bridge every morning and kept walking around it until evening. Finally the captain of the guards, who had been watching him, asked in a kindly way whether he was looking for something or waiting for somebody. The man told him of the dream which had brought him here from a far way country. The captain laughed: "And so to please the dream, you poor fellow wore out your shoes to come here! As for having faith in dreams, if I had any, I should have gone to Krakow and dig for treasure under the stove in the room of a Jew— Eizik the son of Yekel. That was the name, Eizik the son of Yekel! I can just imagine what that would be like. I would have to try every house over there, where one half of the

Jews are named Eizik and the other half are named Yekel!"
And the captain laughed again. At that point, Eizik the son
of Yekel smiled, bowed, traveled home, dug up the treasure
from under the stove, and built the house of prayer which
is called Eizik, the son of Yekel's, synagogue.[57]

Your treasure, your purpose in life, your goals and dreams,
can be sitting right under your nose, right at home or where
you "work" today. If you wish to be great at all, you must
begin where you are with who you are and what you are. My
message is not to change jobs and go off on a quest around the
world for your purpose. In fact, I am still heavily involved in
dentistry—my home. The message of this story is that there
are treasures at home, where you work now. If you wish to
be great anywhere, you must first be great in your own home.

Path Principles

* The path to happiness HEALS us as it: Helps Empower Acts of Loving Service.

* To re-meta-member is to remember our metaphysical purpose and connect with timeless values.

* The Timeless Values Connection
    * Timeless = Freedom
    * Values = Responsibility
    * Connection = Purpose

* Time is a blessing from God empowering us with an arena for changing and becoming more than we are today.

* Your personal purpose is to discover a way of serving others that:
    * Aligns and connect with timeless values, soulfulness, and wisdom.
    * You find meaningful.
    * Others value.
    * Gives you joy.
    * You do well.

* Your purpose in business is your USP, your Unique Solution to my Problem. It is the answer to three questions:
    1. What is the problem that you solve?
    2. What is your systematic solution to the problem?
    3. What makes you unique and different from other businesses? (Why should I use you)

— CHAPTER 7: —
ACT WITH LOVE

Path Prescription #7: The Sacred Path of Serving Others

There is a story that, when the world was young, two brothers shared a field and a mill. Each night they divided evenly the grain that they ground together during the day. Now, as it happened, one of the brothers lived alone; the other had a wife and a large family. One day, the single brother thought to himself: "It isn't really fair that we divide the grain evenly. I have only myself to care for, but my brother has children to feed." So each night he secretly took some of his grain to his brother's granary to see that he was never without.

But the married brother said to himself one day, "It isn't really fair that we divide the grain evenly, because I have children to provide for me in my old age, but my brother has no one. What will he do when he is old?" So every night he secretly took some of *his* grain to his brother's granary. As a result, both of them always found their supply of grain mysteriously replenished each morning.

Then, one night the brothers met each other halfway between

the two houses, suddenly realized what had been happening, and embraced each other in love. The story is that God witnessed their meeting and proclaimed, "This is a holy place, a place of love, and here it is that my temple shall be built." And so it was. The holy place, where God is made known, is a place where human beings discover each other in love."[58]

You can have such a place at work & at home.

This is an amazing story combining love, holiness, and happiness. Loving actions by the brothers led to feelings of love. Love the value, as a verb, precedes love, the feeling. Acts of love (acts of holiness) empowered the brothers to transform an ordinary place into an extraordinary place—a holy place. Through our acts of love we can transform parts of the space-time box from ordinary to extraordinary. We can fill the darkness of space with the light of love. Through our acts of love, we can connect to the hidden God, the Power and **Loving** Greater Than Ourselves, and bring Him back. Love HEALS. It **H**elps **E**mpower **A**cts of **L**oving **S**ervice.

In the book of the Exodus, when it came time to build a portable temple, the Tabernacle, God said: "Let them make me a holy space, and I will dwell within them (Exodus 25:8)." Pay close attention to this statement. It should read, "Let them make me a holy space, and I will dwell within **it**." The lesson is that when we do acts of love, holy acts that create a holy space, God dwells within **us** more than in that space. God dwelling within us leads to joy and inner peace—happiness. Through holiness we come to Shalom and we achieve happiness. *Your Path to Happiness* is a process of holiness.

Naomi Remen has pointed out, "A human being is not a mechanism. A human being is an opportunity for the infinite to manifest itself—this is holiness."[59] We are not only physical beings having a spiritual experience, but we are also spiritual beings having a human experience. Spirituality and holiness are brought into this world through us. We are God's messengers, His business partners, and His partners in the business of life. We are the conduits of the light from the Power and Loving Greater Than Ourselves.

God created mankind in his image. This is a bit strange, because after all, God has no image. The idea here is that God transcends nature and this physical ST box of ours. Although we are physically a part of this material world, we also transcend nature because we are in the image, the shadow, of God. We have a human soul. Our soul is spiritual. Our soul has an awareness of the metaphysical, of a balanced harmonic unity, and of a Power and Loving Greater Than Ourselves. We can use that soul to choose to connect to God's metaphysical Light and to His timeless values. Holiness is the process of taking those timeless values and, in an act of Love, returning back into our world, our Life, and performing acts of service (Love) for others. The result is increased joy and inner peace, happiness—ShaLom for us and for others at work and at home.

Acts of love are quantum units of holiness. We become holy through these acts. As we have said before, while spirituality is an awareness of the sacred, of the existence of the Power and Loving Greater Than Ourselves, holiness is the process of connecting to the sacred and using timeless sacred values in our productive lives as we serve others. The resulting process is a Sacred Path of Serving Others.

Holiness is separating for the purpose of connecting to some higher purpose or meaning. We then bring that purpose and meaning into our productive daily lives. Notice the paradox—separating to connect. Separate from the ordinary to connect with the extraordinary. We are separating from the physical, from pure materialism, and connecting to the metaphysical. For example, when a man and a woman separate themselves from others, and in a promise of fidelity connect to each other through acts of love, this is a holy act. They are separating for the purpose of connecting to some higher purpose or meaning. In Hebrew, the marriage service is called Kiddushin. The root of the word is "kadosh", which means "holy". The very service itself is a process of holiness. The couple is separating to connect!

The wedding is not merely a secular contract between two people. It is a covenant. As Robert Kane points out, "Turning it into a sacred bond means that their union has significance that goes beyond themselves linking them to the wider community, and even to the whole of creation."[60] While separating from others, a man and a woman can connect in harmony, becoming one, and miraculously creating another one. Those acts of love can bring forth new life into this world. Thus, a family is born. A harmonious family can create a neighborhood, which can in turn create a city, a state, a nation, a world, and even a universe, all playing a symphony of love.

Another example of separating for the purpose of connecting to some higher purpose or meaning is practicing ethical behavior at work. When I practiced clinical dentistry, before I cemented a crown (a cap) in a person's mouth I took care to make sure that the fit was excellent. If it was not an excellent fit, this could lead to all kinds of problems in the future. However, it would often take years before the crown would fail, and the patient might never know the real cause. The Power and Loving Greater Than Ourselves and I would be the only two entities in the universe who would know the truth. By re-doing any poorly fitting crown I was actualizing holiness. In choosing to separate from the profane, unethical act (cementing a bad crown) and connecting to God through ethical values (redoing the crown) I became holy. In these cases, not only was I connecting with God, but I was connecting with the patient. I was connecting with another human being who has intrinsic value. Because I valued that human being, it was my responsibility to serve that person well. By serving that other person ethically, I separated from the unethical for the purpose of connecting to some higher purpose or meaning.

Here the higher purpose and meaning included love, human worth, and God's values—that is to say, doing the right thing. These are examples of covenant as opposed to contract. Contracts are about protecting one's interests. They are about power and law, and more especially they are about enforcement of the law through the power of the state. Contracts operate over a fixed period of time and the parties involved remain as separate entities. Many of our interactions with other people are contractual interactions.

Covenantal relationships are quite different. Unlike contracts which are about interests, covenants are about identity. They turn a group of individuals into a collective. They take **you** and **me** and turn it into **we**. In a covenant, people come together and are able to do what they cannot do by themselves. The key element here is not power, but is a promise—the giving of one's word to another. It is about the trust that is expressed in that interaction. It is about a handshake, not a contract.

Trust depends on my giving my word and keeping it. A covenant is made when free people who respect each other's individual freedom commit themselves, through promise and through giving their word, to work together for some end. Covenant maintains independence, while at the same time empowering interdependence. Through covenants we build loving, service based relationships. We turn ordinary relationships into holy relationships.

When it comes to customer service, the question is, "Do

you act with your customer in a contractual or covenantal manner?" Here's an example from my experience. One summer I needed a brand new air conditioner, so I went to the company that had the best reputation in the area. They installed top-of-the-line unit that cost $5,000. Of course this came with a guarantee:five years on the parts and one year on the labor. About three years later, we noticed one day that the air was not cooling the house. I called the company and a service technician was sent out. After charging $750 he told me that he had probably fixed a leak, but it was possible that there were other problems.

He was correct. Two weeks later the same problem repeated itself. A second technician was sent out. The readings were the same as before the first service man had started. In two weeks we had lost all pressure. His solution was that they should return and aggressively search and test the lines to find out if the problem was in the coil inside the furnace, inside the house, or in the compressor unit outside the house. That procedure could cost up to $1,000 for the labor. Once the site of the leak was located, they could then fix that problem. Of course that part would not cost anything because I was within the five years of the guarantee on parts. Unfortunately, the one year labor guarantee was not going to do me much good in the third year. So there would be an additional labor fee to put in the guaranteed part which I was told could be as much as $1,000 more. To add insult to injury I was charged $90 for this visit and the information. In other words, I had bought the top-of-the-line unit from a top-of-the-line company for $5,000 and now three years later I was apparently going to need to pay close to $3,000 for a leak! Not only that, but apparently they couldn't do this until the following week. We're talking almost a week waiting for an air conditioner to be fixed in August in Chicago.

I was not a happy camper and called an alternative company. The technician was at the house within 30 minutes and diagnosed several alternatives. One of the problems was that the first company had possibly put the wrong kind of chemical agent in the system. If that was so, then it would cost me $800, and if any other work needed to be performed the maximum charge would be $1,200. We concluded the agreement with a handshake. He returned on the very next day and his $800 repair worked just fine.

What we have here is a difference between a contractual relationship and a covenantal relationship. The first company was following a strict contractual relationship. The contract said very clearly one year guarantee on labor. They stuck by that contract precisely. My understanding had been that our relationship would extend beyond the contract, because I thought I had made a covenantal agreement with this company. That's the whole idea of customer service. A covenantal customer service relationship goes beyond the legal agreement with your customer. It means standing behind your work and exceeding expectations. Legally, they were correct, but from a covenantal expectation, customer service standpoint they failed miserably. They lost a customer, and have now found themselves on the wrong side of a story in a book about service. The second company did the work on a handshake, charged me $665 (even though we had agreed to $800), and came back later to verify that everything was still okay at no charge. That is a covenantal relationship.

Are your relationships with your customers purely contractual or are they covenantal? Is your customer just a means to your ends (sales and profit) or is servicing your customer your purpose in life? Is your purpose to be sure that you don't get burned in any of your relationships or is your purpose to serve people who have a need that you can fill? Is your relationship with your customers at the level of "you and me" or is it at the level of "we?" Covenants are about relationships between people who share values and exchange value. Thinking about your customers in a covenantal, rather than contractual, relationship HEALS your relationship with your customers. It **Helps Empower Acts of Loving Service.**

Loving Others

We love others by being of service to them. *Your Path to Happiness* is a Sacred Path of Serving Others. Let's first focus on what we mean by "love" and then focus on what we mean by "others."

Love is the primary healing value. As we learned, there is a

Universal Whole-Parts-Whole Process. The act of our birth is an act of separation. We were integrated, whole, and at one in the metaphysical realm. At birth, we were separated from that wholeness and came into this world of uncertainty, paradox, and of parts. God is hidden in the parts and it is hard to find Him. We become disconnected individuals, we are alone, and we feel broken. Through connection with another soul, we are healed and made whole. Plato believed that **love is connection with another soul**.[61] I believe that "other" soul is either that of another human being or it is the Power and Loving Greater Than Ourselves. By connecting with another person, we reconnect indirectly to the Power and Loving Greater Than Ourselves through the human soul that is found deep inside that other human being.

There are also ways of connecting directly to the Power and Loving Greater Than Ourselves. Loving connection heals us. While we are alive, we never fully arrive, we are never cured. Entropy, life's pain and problems, strikes again. Life is a terminal condition. We all die and there is no cure. However, through loving connections we can heal.

The best definition of love than I have ever come across is that of M. Scott Peck in his book *The Road Less Traveled*, **"I define love thus: The will to extend one's self for the purpose of nurturing one's own or another's spiritual growth."**[62] Read that again, and again, and again. It is worth the effort. Let's take it apart, analyze it, and then put it back together.

The will: Love is an act of will. Your will is your power to choose your own actions. Freedom of will implies freedom of choice. It is the power of control that your mind has over your actions. We choose to love. Love is a verb—an action word. The love we refer to here is a value, *not* a feeling. For many people love is only a feeling over which they have no control. They "fall" in love. They claim that they just can't help themselves. In other words, they are a victim of love. Like any victim, they become a slave to their victimizer. They lose themselves in the other person. Most importantly, they lose their ability to make independent choices based on values. The problem here is that they let the feeling of love precede loving action.

There is nothing wrong with a feeling of love. However, feelings must remain secondary to values. They must be processed through our beliefs, knowledge, wisdom, and our soul. We must climb the Ladder of Learning. Loving feelings are what follow from loving actions and acts of service. Love is a conscious choice that we make to act on purpose.

To extend one's self: Love is difficult. It requires significant effort and work. Most of all it requires time, which is a significant and limited resource. Relationships do not simply happen. They require nurturing and care. Love is risky. After exerting much effort, many acts of service, and spending much time in a relationship, you are always at risk that you will not be loved back. Rather than healing from your human wounds, there is the risk that by failing at love, one can become even more broken.

For the purpose of nurturing one's own or another's: It is important to love yourself as well as others. We will cover this momentarily.

For the purpose of nurturing one's own or another's spiritual growth: Love is acting on purpose. The purpose of love is not to feel good, but rather it is for spiritual growth. It is only through spiritual growth, through *Your Path to Happiness*, that you can heal from your human condition. Life is growth. Spiritual life requires spiritual growth, which, in turn, requires purposeful thinking and acting. By loving, serving, and connecting to others we empower the spiritual growth that leads to the achievement of happiness.

Therefore love can be defined as the will to extend one's self for the purpose of nurturing one's own or another's spiritual growth. Love is a purposeful choice that is difficult and risky. Its purpose is to achieve spiritual growth and spiritual healing for ourselves and others, both at work and at home.

Now let's discuss what we mean by "others." We can serve three "others." The highest "other" is the Power Greater Than Ourselves—God. The second "other" consists of other people. The final "other" may not be obvious at first. Think about it, what other "other" could there be? Pay attention to your thinking. Who is it that is thinking? When I think about thinking, an interesting thing happens. I seem to think about myself or see myself as someone actually separate from myself. It is as if my mind is separate from me in some way. Or even better, my mind is the real me, the eternal me. That "eternal me" seems to be able to view, to judge, and to command the "present me." In other words I can see myself as an "other"!

Human beings have self-awareness. We have souls. We can judge our actions. We can command ourselves to change by decision and will. So the first "other" that we must serve is ourselves! One can't serve water from an empty pitcher. We must fill our pitcher first, and once that is done we can serve others. The same concept holds true for the oxygen mask that drops in front of you on a plane. You must put a mask on yourself first, then on others. You cannot help others if you have no oxygen.

Two thousand years ago, Rabbi Hillel put it this way, "If I am not for myself, who will be for me? If I am only for myself what am I? And if not now, when?"[63] In other words, I must take care of myself first. I am responsible for myself. However, once I've taken care of myself I must help others. If I only care about myself and do not help others, what kind of person am I? A life lived caring only about myself is neither a sacred path nor a path to happiness. The last point that Hillel makes, "and if not now, when?" in recent years has been rephrased, "just do it". Rabbi Hillel had Nike beat by 2,000 years.

The concept of three others appears in the Bible as well. Love of God is found in Deuteronomy 6:5; "And you shall love the Lord your God with all your heart, and with all your soul, and with all your might." Love of other people can be found in Leviticus 19:18 "And you shall love your neighbor as yourself." Now if you look closely at this verse you will notice that loving your neighbor requires the understanding of loving yourself. From here we see that you must love yourself first, and only then shall you love your neighbor. The trick here is to understand how to balance serving three others.

You must begin with yourself. You must love yourself. The purpose of loving yourself is not to make you feel good. Remember, the purpose of loving yourself is to nurture your own spiritual growth. How can you best nurture that growth? You nurture your spiritual growth by taking responsibility for your own life. You must accept the reality that your present conditions are the result of your thinking, decisions that you've made, and actions that you have taken until today. By taking responsibility, you begin with yourself and straighten yourself out before you work with others.

Martin Buber in his book, *The Way of Man*, tells this story: "Rabbi Hayyim of Zans had married his son to the daughter of Rabbi Eliezer. The day after the wedding he visited the father of the bride and said, "Now that we are related I feel close to you and can tell you what is eating up my heart. Look! My hair and beard have grown white, and I have not yet atoned!' "Oh my friend," replied Rabbi Eliezer, "you are thinking only of yourself. How about forgetting about yourself and thinking of the world?"[64]

This seems to contradict what we just said that one should begin with oneself. Here we are told that a man should forget himself. To understand, one need only ask one question: For what purpose? For what purpose am I to be responsible? For what purpose am I to choose my own particular path? The answer is, "Not for my own sake alone." That is why the previous injunction was to begin with oneself. Yes, you should begin with yourself, but do not end with yourself. In the story, Rabbi Eliezer is saying, "Do not keep worrying about what you have done wrong. Apply the energy that your soul is now wasting on past failures to planning and achieving your purpose here. You should not be occupied with yourself but with the world. You should be focusing on a particular mission, or on a particular value, for the fulfillment of which you were put in this world."[65]

The order becomes:

1. Love yourself. Foster your spiritual growth by taking responsibility. Begin with yourself, but do not end with yourself.
2. Love others. Foster the spiritual growth of others by

being of service to them. You are here to be of service to others in some unique way.

3. Love God. By serving others you are indirectly serving God. God put each of us here for a unique purpose, and by serving each other with the unique talents and abilities granted to us by God, we do His work. We are the conduits of God's light. We heal each other's wounds and help solve each other's problems. We are His messengers. We are His business partners—partners in this business of life.

The Golden Rule

The preceding discussion focused on the biblical passage: "Love your neighbor as yourself." This statement, love your neighbor as yourself, is an early formulation of the Golden Rule. Let's look at this in more detail.

Love = Action. First, don't harm others. Second, help others to grow spiritually.

Your Neighbor = We are all human beings made in the image of God. We are therefore all created equal—of equal human worth and value.

As Yourself = Treat your neighbor as a person, not a thing. As Martin Buber has pointed out, one should have an I/Thou relationship, not an I/It relationship with another person. He, too, is a person—an end in and of himself. He is not simply an object—a means towards your ends.

The Golden Rule is an excellent tool for understanding how to serve others. It is simple without being simplistic. This can be seen from a famous story from the Talmud.[66]

> A person came to Rabbi Shamai and asked the Rabbi to explain to him the entire corpus of Jewish knowledge while the questioner stood on one foot. Rabbi Shamai, who worked as a builder, grabbed a hammer and ran the gentleman off, all the while exclaiming how silly the concept was. The person then went to Rabbi Hillel and asked him the same thing. Rabbi Hillel immediately answered, "Do not do to others what you would not want done to you. The rest is just commentary—go learn." And the questioner did.

Rabbi Hillel gave the negative formulation of the Golden rule, "Love your neighbor as yourself."

Robert Kane, in the tape series: *The Quest for Meaning, Values, Ethics and the Modern Experience*[67] and Tom Morris, in his book: *If Aristotle Ran General Motors*,[68] both point out the universal nature of the Golden Rule ("Do unto others as you would have them do unto you"). It has been a central principle of most of the major religious traditions of mankind. Various formulations of it can be found around the world.

Confucius (China) in his Analex said, "Do not do unto others what you would not want them to do unto you."

Taoism (China): "View your neighbor's gain as your own gain, and your neighbor's loss as your own loss."

Hinduism (India): In the Mahavarata there is a chapter called the Bavarata Gita (the song of God) which says this: "All of your duties are included in this: Do nothing to others that would pain you if it were done to you." Once again we see the Golden Rule as the sum of all duty.

Buddhism (India:) The Odana Vaga says, "Seek for others the happiness you desire for yourself. Hurt not others with that which pains you."

Zoroastria (Middle East): In the main text of the Zoroastrians it says, "That nature alone is good which refrains from doing unto another whatsoever is not good for itself."

Christianity (Israel): In Matthew (7:12) Jesus says, "All things whatsoever ye would that men should do unto you do ye even so unto them for this is the law and the prophets."

Islam (Saudi Arabia): In the Sunna it says "Let none of you treat his brother in a way he himself would not like to be treated. No one of you is a believer until he loves for his brother what he loves for himself."

The Golden rule is a "lighthouse" that has become a virtually universal guiding principle for serving others. The rule HEALS us. It **Helps Empower Acts of Loving Service.**

It shines **Light** on our **Path** teaching us to **Love** others. Love of others empowers **Life** and reconnects us with the **Power Greater Than Ourselves.** We become whole and we have **ShaLom.** Life in this world is a journey through the parts in search of wholeness, joy, and inner peace—happiness (shalom).

Serving Others

Rabbi Moshe Leib of Sasov learned to love when he went to an inn and heard one drunken peasant ask another, "Do you love me?" "Certainly I love you," replied the second. "I love you like a brother." But the first shook his head and insisted, "You don't love me. You don't know what I lack. You don't know what I need." The second peasant fell into sullen silence, but Rabbi Moshe Leib understood: "To know the need of men and to bear the burden of their sorrow—that is the true love of men."[69]

To love others is to serve others, but to serve others you must both value others and bring value to others. That in turn requires connection through communication. I must do more than just feel for the other person. I must listen to the other person. I must hear the other person, and only then can I know the other person. I cannot love, serve, or help another person until I know what that person lacks and what that person needs. That can only come through listening, hearing, and understanding others. We are here to:

Solve problems
Heal pain
Address needs
Look to satisfy wants
Overcome challenges
Make opportunities

Gerhard Gschwandtner said, "Your customers do not care how much you know until they know how much you care."[70] You show people how much you care by giving them time and attention. Time is a great gift because it is a fixed resource. Once you give time, you can never get it back. The more time you give something, the more value you place on it. If you value a person, you give that person your time.

Focused attention and active listening are other great gifts that can connect you with the spirit of another person. You cannot help another person to grow spiritually if you do not connect with their spirit.

In their book *The Spirituality of Imperfection*, Ernest Kurtz and Katherine Ketcham tell us the story of a nursing home resident who captures both the importance of listening thoroughly and the despair that occurs when no one is available or willing to listen:

"Heard... if they only understood how important it is that we be heard! I can take being in a nursing home. It's really all right, with a positive attitude. My daughter has her hands full, three kids and a job. She visits regularly. I understand."

"But most people here...they just want to tell their story. That's what they have to give, don't you see? And it's a precious thing to them. It's their life they want to give. You'd think people would understand what it means to us...to give our lives in a story."

"So we listen to each other. Most of what goes on here is people listening to each other's stories. People who work here consider that to be...filling time. If they only knew—if they'd just take a minute to listen!"[71]

How can you listen to others more effectively? The best system is **Active Listening**. Many people talk about active listening. Here are the steps that I use:

Listen without interruption. Listen attentively to what the person has to say. Make eye contact and stay focused for as much of the time as possible. Do not try to formulate a quick answer at this point. Instead try to see yourself in their shoes. Try to understand their paradigm.

Pause. This step is the key to becoming an active listener.

Pausing accomplishes several things. First of all, a person may not be finished speaking, but may be only taking a break. By pausing and allowing the speaker to continue without interruption, you show how much you care. Second, by pausing you demonstrate the validity of the speaker's point of view. Pausing shows that you're thinking about what was said. Third, pausing gives you a chance to formulate your feedback and your response. Finally, pausing gives you an opportunity to connect to the Power and Loving Greater Than Ourselves in this moment of encounter. This will be explained further in Chapter 8.

Feedback. Do not begin with your own response! Hold off on any response until the other person validates your perception of what he or she has said.

> **Feedback emotion.** Summarize for the other person how you understand them to be feeling. It is best to begin with emotions because they drive decisions. Do not comment positively or negatively on the emotion. Allow the other person to feel entitled to her feelings.

> **Feedback content.** Restate in your own words the point that the other person is making.

Verification. Ask the person to verify that you understand both the emotion and the content of the statements. Go back to listening without interruption and pause. If the speaker verifies that you have gotten it right, you can move on to responding. If you did not get the emotion and content exactly right, try to restate it or if necessary ask some questions to clarify matters. Never move on to your response without verifying that you have gotten the emotion and the content to the speaker's satisfaction.

Respond. At this point you can give your response to the other person's comments.

Please notice that the last thing that you do here is respond. Our nature is to want to respond immediately. We want to be understood, and we feel that if we can only get a chance to explain ourselves to someone, that person will understand us and then will agree with us. Nothing could be further from the truth. Stephen Covey in his book, *The 7 Habits of Highly Effective People*, beautifully articulates the best concept I have ever found for excellent interpersonal communication:

"Seek first to understand, then to be understood."[72]

Active listening to another person is an act of love. Think about it. What you would really like to do first is to be understood. You would like to be talking, not listening. However, in seeking first to understand, you must listen to another intensively until he/she feels understood emotionally, as well as intellectually. In giving feedback as to your understanding of what the speaker is feeling and thinking, you show that you care. In refraining from offering any response until after verifying that you understand these feelings and the speaker's thinking, you are demonstrating that you respect and value this person. This is an act of love, but it is very difficult. Clearly you must use the will to extend yourself for the purpose of nurturing another's spiritual growth. Through nurturing another's spiritual growth, you also nurture your own spiritual growth. Kurtz and Ketcham bring a story that shows the difficulty of true act of listening.

> *"When a man whose marriage was in trouble sought his advice, the Master said, 'You must learn to listen to your wife.' The man took this advice to heart and returned after a month to say that he had learned to listen to every word his wife was saying. Said the Master with a smile, 'Now go home and listen to every word she isn't saying.'"*[73]

Active listening is an act of love that can bring you happiness at work and at home. To be of true service, we must connect with those whom we serve by paying attention to them. Our listening cannot be focused on technique. We must listen with attention and intention. We must listen to what is said and what is not said. Body language speaks to us as well. Only after we truly understand another can we begin to diagnose their unique problems, suffering, needs, wants, and challenges. Only after a proper diagnosis can one move on to treatment. Only when a customer or a family member feels that you have a true diagnosis of their unique issues will you be able to respond effectively with influencing or problem-solving.

Kurtz and Ketcham point out that the intentionality between human beings can be understood by comparing a wink to a blink.[74] They look alike. But a blink is unintended. Its purpose is personal and individual, simply to lubricate the eye. A wink, however, has a different purpose. A wink conveys an intention and is therefore specifically directed toward another. The wink can succeed as a wink only if it is perceived by the other as a wink and not as a blink. Our deepest human behaviors are fundamentally intentional. It takes two to wink. With a wink the two can form a link that can lead to a community. Within a community we can serve each other leading to joy and inner peace, unity and wholeness, in a word shalom.

Active Listening Steps

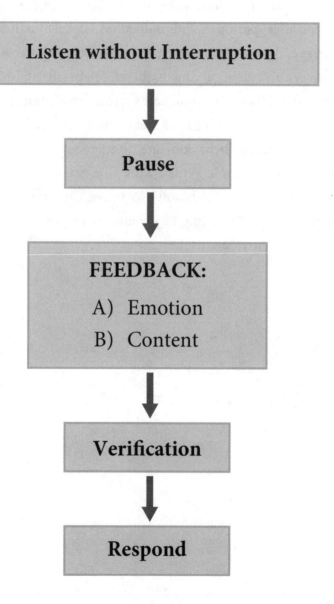

Path Principles

* Holiness is separating for the purpose of connecting to some higher purpose or meaning. We then bring that purpose and meaning into our productive daily lives.

* Through covenants we build loving, service-based relationships. We turn ordinary relationships into holy relationships.

* M. Scott Peck: "I define love thus: The will to extend one's self for the purpose of nurturing one's own or another's spiritual growth."

* We serve three others:
  1. Ourselves
  2. Other people
  3. The Power and Loving Greater Than Ourselves

* The Golden Rule: Love your neighbor as yourself.

* Gerhard Gschwandtner has said, "Your customers do not care how much you know until they know how much you care."
  * Is your relationship with your customers at the level of "you and me" or is it at the level of "we?"
  * Is your relationship with your customers contractual or covenantal?

* Stephen Covey: "Seek first to understand, then to be

understood."

* Steps for Active Listening:
  1. Listen without interruption.
  2. Pause.
  3. Feedback emotion and content.
  4. Verification.
  5. Respond.

— CHAPTER 8: —

LIFE IS A JOURNEY THROUGH MOMENTS OF ENCOUNTER

Path Prescription #8: Moments of Encounter

Life Is a Journey through moments of encounter along *Your Path to Happiness*. I first learned about moments of encounter and choosing a better path on a trip to Coronado near San Diego. The first day I was there, I went out for a run, which was okay. It was interesting in that I ran around the bay where military vessels were docked. All in all, it was an ordinary run. The next day, I started my run on the same path, unaware that there was any other way to go. As I was running, however, I noticed a dark tunnel and ran past it. For the next moment or two I could not get my mind off of the tunnel. The tunnel ran under the highway. I wondered where it went and whether it was safe or dangerous. I had to turn back and give it a try.

The tunnel was dark and made me very nervous. Looking into the depths of the tunnel I could see a small, distinct light. The light called to me and drew me into the tunnel. As

I ran through the tunnel, I could hear cars flying by above me on the highway. Someone else entered the tunnel from the other side and came closer and closer to me. The closer he came, the faster my heartbeat. He passed me by with a smile and a wave. "That was a close one," I thought. I could see the proverbial light at the end of the tunnel. I picked up my speed and came out of the tunnel into the light.

Unbelievable! I had the most incredible sight in front of me—the shore of the Pacific Ocean. The sandy beach extended to my left and right as far as I could see. I ran south for about half an hour, north for about 45 minutes, and back south for 15 minutes. For about an hour and a half I had of one of the greatest runs of my life. For about an hour and a half I had joy and inner peace. I had shalom—happiness.

I had experienced a *moment of encounter*. By appropriately engaging in that moment I was able to actualize happiness. Facing the tunnel was my moment of encounter. I had come across the tunnel, I had happened upon the tunnel, and I had encountered the tunnel. That great run was only possible because I was willing to journey through the tunnel. The tunnel was a hidden messenger. The message of the moment was, "Have the courage to try a new path."

Take a risk. Take the first step and choose to search for light. Light is a healing value. Pursue that value. By choosing to pass through the tunnel in the moment of encounter, to seek out the light at the end of the tunnel, I was able to take an ordinary run and turn it into an extraordinary run.

The run was extraordinary because it connected me to several of my key values. I value the beauty of nature, the magnificent world that God created, health and fitness, and I enjoy physical activity. While running in a natural setting, I can go into the silence and listen to the small still voice calling me to fulfill my purpose—my primary healing value.

In this case, while running, I was able to connect to my spirituality and heal from the pain and problems that I was facing. What problems was I facing? Well it turns out this run happened just six months after my bicycle accident. It was still early in the treatment of my depression. This was one of the first moments when I felt whole again. I felt balanced and connected to the harmonic unity of the universe—shalom. That extraordinary run gave me joy and inner peace—happiness. That possibility, to create an extraordinary moment and experience happiness, is always present in our lives.

What moments make your life extraordinary? What messengers are hidden in the moments of your life? What messages do they bring you? What is your path to happiness? What tunnel must you pass through to get to the extraordinary rewards on the other side? What desert must you cross to get to the Promised Land? What moments of encounter must you experience along your path to happiness?

Life is a journey through moments of encounter, and these are special pieces of space and time. Moments of encounter are tests, challenges, or opportunities to learn and grow. Life is about spiritual growth. Every moment is a blessing. Every instant is a gift filled with positive as well as negative potential. Our job is to find and actualize the positive potential in any moment.

Inside every moment a miracle is hiding. Life is a journey, a quest for wholeness, joy, and inner peace—for achieving moments of happiness. Moments of encounter are the instants in the space time box where we do our work while God's messengers do their work. The key to any moment of encounter is how we choose to respond to those messengers with their messages. Life is lived through events or encounters with the outside world (stimulus). More specifically, life is lived through relationships—encounters with others in the world. Each encounter becomes part of your life's story. Through the choices that you make in those moments of encounter (response), your story evolves.

Making better choices in any moment of encounter leads you to more moments of happiness at work and at home. A simple customer complaint is a moment of encounter. By responding to the challenge in any moment by being of service to others and creating value for others you can help create extraordinary moments, holy moments, for yourself and for others. When one of your children shares a problem with you, this is a moment of encounter. Loving that child requires actively listening in that instant. Choosing better responses in moments of encounter requires training and practice climbing the Ladder of Learning and using the values from the three lessons of learning—*freedom, responsibility,* and *purpose*—as a guide through those moments.

Freedom empowers me to recognize that whatever conditions I face and whatever challenges I find in any moment of encounter, I can choose my response to those conditions. I have choice. My choices may be limited and difficult, but I must always search for messengers with a message of what choices are available and which choices lead to happiness. We always have a choice.

Responsibility is the ability to accept what is and choose a response that leads to happiness in any moment of encounter. Holiness is the process of making responsible spiritual choices and acting on those choices in moments of encounter— moments in your daily productive life. Regardless of your situation, you can think and act responsibly. You can always search for truth and do the right thing. What is the right thing in any given moment of encounter? That can be determined by thinking and acting on purpose—by using the four healing values to reconnect to your purpose.

Purpose is why you exist. Overcoming challenges and achieving happiness is only possible by purposeful thinking and acting in moments of encounter. Thinking and acting on purpose HEALS us. It Helps Empower Acts of Loving Service. Remember that customer service leads to **SHALOM** because we: **S**olve problems, **H**eal pain, **A**ddress needs, **L**ook to satisfy wants, **O**vercome challenges, and **M**ake opportunities at work and at home. Staying on purpose helps us to choose better responses in moments of encounter.

Of these three values, responsibility is the key to moments of encounter. For me, the classic moment of encounter occurs in the Garden of Eden (Genesis 2-3). All other moments of encounter follow from this first moment. I agree with Rabbi Lawrence Kushner that the Garden was a setup.[75] Think about it. You can eat the fruit of all the trees in the garden except the one with the luscious, gorgeous, delicious looking fruit right smack in the middle of the garden. You can't miss that if you tried, because it is in your way no matter where you go, and you can't avoid seeing it every single day. But *do not* eat from that tree. That is a setup, pure and simple.

Here's a similar set up. Imagine telling your two teenage boys the following, "Guys, I'm leaving on my African Safari today. Remember I'll be completely unreachable. They are going to helicopter us into the base and helicopter us out of there one week later. In the meantime, here are the keys to the Ferrari. I'm putting them right here, smack in the middle of the kitchen on the table. Do not touch the keys." In most universe lines, the keys probably stayed put. But in our universe things get interesting. We take the keys and we eat from the tree. That was the point. It was a setup. We were supposed to eat.

Why the setup? Because the point was *not* that they did something wrong. God's message was, "Of course you did something wrong. You are human." You lose because you are human. At some point you were bound to do something wrong. Adam and Eve were ashamed, and so they hid from God. There is a crazy concept. Hiding from God? But the two were young—theoretically only a couple of hours old. They had not really thought this completely through and they thought they could get away with it. When they realized that they had gotten caught, they were hiding from God. Let it go.

Now here comes the real test. Here comes the whole purpose of the setup. God comes into the garden and asks the key question of life. Unfortunately this question, which in the original Hebrew Bible is one word, is often misinterpreted. The usual translation is: "Where are you?" That would be the translation of the Hebrew word "ayfoh," but that is not the word that is used here. Instead the Hebrew word used is "Ayekah," which literally translates to "Where Here?" The figurative translation is **'Where do you stand?"** Where is your here? What do you stand for? Can you take a stand? Who are you? What is your "So That___!" What is your purpose? What God is really asking is: "In this moment of encounter can you choose an extraordinary response? **Are you responsible?"**

Responsibility is the name of the human game. Adam and Eve were human and therefore, at some point, they were bound to make a mistake. Their moment of encounter began with this mistake. Eating from the tree was not the mistake. It began the game, which was not about making a mistake. It was about the response they gave to the mistake. They hid in shame, and other each other they did blame.

What was God looking for? He was looking for human acceptance of accountability and responsibility for his or her actions. Remember, you lose because you are human. You win because you are you. You can take individual responsibility in any moment of encounter. You can add some unique value or some unique service to this world in any moment of encounter. That was the response that God wanted: we are responsible. What did he get? He got ordinary shame and blame.

God asked, "Ayekah? Where do you stand? What are you made of?" Adam answered, "I am made of shame and I am hiding." God gave him another chance to choose responsibility and asked, "Did you eat from the tree?" Again Adam refused to choose to accept responsibility. Adam said that the woman made him do it. Eve said that the snake made her do it. Blame, blame, blame!

At this point God said, "Okay, everybody out of the pool." They are sent out of the garden. All that Adam and Eve needed to do was to take responsibility. All they had to do was to say they were wrong, that they were sorry, and that they would be better. All they had to do was make an act of repentance, but instead they were irresponsible. Only responsible people can live in the extraordinary location in space-time called the Garden of Eden.

Our life is the story of our quest to get back to the metaphorical Garden. It is a quest for becoming whole once again. We exist in this world as separate parts— individuals. Deep in our genes, deep in our human story, is the easy and ordinary choice—blame. Blame protects us from dealing with other individuals and other parts. Can we ever accept full accountability and responsibility before and, more importantly, after our mistakes and failures? Yes we can.

Lesson one taught us that we always have freedom. As we pointed out previously, Viktor Frankl explains that "To be sure, a human being is a finite thing, and his freedom is restricted. It is not freedom from conditions, but it is freedom to take a stand toward the conditions."[76] In other words, we are not free to choose our conditions and so we should accept our conditions. We are, however, completely free to choose our response to those conditions. We can choose an extraordinary response. **Accept what is and choose your extraordinary response in any moment of encounter.**

Frankl goes on to say: "Man is ultimately self-determining...[77] In the concentration camps...we watched and witnessed some of our comrades behaved like swine while others behaved like saints. Man has both potentialities within himself; which one is actualized depends on decisions but not on conditions... Man is that being who invented the gas chambers of Auschwitz; however, he is also that being who entered those gas chambers upright, with the Lord's Prayer or the Shema Yisrael on his lips."[78]

We are always free to choose our response. Remember the grandfather and the German soldiers. **Everyone always has a choice**. We have freedom. Adam and Eve were given the gift of the freedom to eat from any tree. This included the freedom to disobey God and eat fruit from the one forbidden tree. That act, however, had consequences. In their moment of encounter at the tree, the tree was a messenger with the message that along with freedom comes responsibility.

Since our freedom comes from God, God can limit our freedom. Our responsibility is to recognize that timeless truth and act accordingly. You lose because you are human. Humans make mistakes and at times act irresponsibly. You win because you are you. You can accept responsibility. You can even accept responsibility after you make a mistake. You have the ability to repair mistakes. You can accept responsibility for problems and, by using your unique talents and abilities, find solutions to those problems. Adam and Eve did not accept responsibility for their actions. They were sent out of the garden into the "real" world. That "real" world is our world. We do not live in the Garden of Eden! Life is challenging and painful. It is filled with moments of encounter—moments that challenge us in our journey through life. In those moments, will we blame or will we take responsibility?

In my business and my life, I must choose between blame and responsibility. The ordinary answer to the "Why me?" question is "Because____." We want to fill in the blank so that we can blame. Blaming makes us feel better in that moment. In any moment of encounter we find it easier to focus on the causes of our problems, rather than on the solutions to our problems. Solutions require further action, and this is usually difficult action. It is far easier to blame some other cause for our feelings and for us to play the victim.

When a customer complains, when employees argue, or when profitability goes down, the easy path is to feel victimized. The underlying expectation here is that life should be without any suffering. Life, the universe, owes me that much. I'm entitled to it because I have rights, especially the right to feel good at all times. This focus on feelings, on rights without responsibilities, and on past causes, never leads to inner peace. Irresponsibility never leads to happiness, either. The only path to inner peace is to move from a focus of "What caused my problem" to "How can I solve my problem?" This requires a new and extraordinary way of thinking about the question itself: "Why me?"

The extraordinary response begins by freely accepting responsibility. The extraordinary way of thinking about our question, "Why me?" requires a change in our focus from feelings to values. The question changes to the point where it is not even the same question. Instead of asking "Why do I ever suffer?" the question becomes "Why do I exist?" The extraordinary answer becomes "So That___!" I fill in the blank with a meaningful purpose that I must discover based on my values.

The entire focus shifts from asking "What does life owe me?" to asking "What do I owe life?" The focus also shifts from the past to the future, from causes to solutions, from a broken unfixable world to a world that we can repair, from our rights to our responsibilities, and from human being to human becoming. As Rabbi Hirsch once noted, "To the exclusiveness of rights, must be added the inclusiveness of love."[79] This requires taking responsibility. In my case, once I took responsibility I then learned that my problems and suffering were *So That* I could become an extraordinary speaker. The power of that purpose overrode the pain of problems that I found in moments of encounter.

Each moment of encounter contains a story. Stories impose meaning and order in the chaos of our lives. Facts are meaningless until you create a story around them. The most important story you will ever tell about yourself is the story that you tell to yourself. Most people live an ordinary story. They never take a journey along *Your Path to Happiness.*

But you can live an extraordinary story. After all, you are the hero, and heroes are never ordinary. What is it about you that is special, unique, heroic, or even epic? What is your extraordinary story? The theme of your story is the purpose of your life. Without purpose your story has no meaning, no direction, or organizing concept. Without a purpose it is all but impossible to overcome challenges in moments of encounter and go on to achieve happiness. With purpose, on the other hand, people do amazing things along their path to achieving happiness. *In any situation we always have the freedom to choose a responsible, purposeful, and extraordinary response.*

Responsibility is the ability to accept what is and choose a response that is extraordinary in a moment of encounter.

A moment of encounter is an opportunity to engage the spiritual potential present in our physical space-time universe.

A moment of encounter is an instant of engagement with the past, present, and future in which we can choose to transform our lives from ordinary to extraordinary (become holy). It is a moment in which we can choose to be happy, choose our path to happiness, and experience moments of happiness.

Responsibility Runs in the Family

Several years ago, we were having dinner with some friends, whose names have been changed to protect their privacy. One of the friends, Sarah, who was sitting next to me, shared a story about an experience she had with her son, Jim. One summer, when he was nine years old, he attended a day camp. One day the camp was going on a field trip with transportation supplied by bus. Jim was never one to instigate trouble, but on this particular day he was sitting next to Tom, a young man who was a trouble maker. Tom brought a bag of rocks aboard the bus. Turning to Jim, he was able to convince him that it would be fun to throw these rocks out the window at passing cars on the highway. At nine years old, it sounded like fun. So Jim and Tom began throwing rocks out the window.

Before they knew it, the police had pulled the bus over to the side of the road. One of the people whose car was hit by a rock, Mr. Thomas, had called the police on his phone. There was some discussion between the policemen, Mr. Thomas, and some counselors. The head counselor came on board the bus and asked who threw rocks out of the window at cars? Jim stood up, Tom remain seated. Jim was removed from the bus, sent back to the camp, and his mother, Sarah, was called. As it turned out, Jim was suspended from the camp for three days. Of course the last of those three days was the day that the camp went to the Cubs baseball game. Jim had looked forward to that game for months.

For most kids that would have been the end of the story. Jim, however, had Sarah for his mother. After arriving home and telling him how disappointed she was, she explained, "We have to make this better." Sarah called Tom's mother, who was not interested in "making this better." She tried to play it all down. "Boys will be boys, let's just let this pass." Sarah disagreed, "I think they need to go to the man's house, offer to pay for what they did, and apologize for what they did." Tom's mother replied, "Count me out." Sara turned to Jim and said, "Well it looks like we will have to do this on our own." Sara put in a call to Mr. Thomas (She had been given his number by the camp.) Sarah identified herself to Mr. Thomas and then asked, "May I please bring my son to your house to apologize for what he has done?" Mr. Thomas agreed. Sarah then turned to face Jim and said, "Tomorrow morning we are going over to the home of the man whose car you hit. You will face him, you will apologize to him, you will offer to pay for the damages to his car, and you will tell him that you will not ever do anything like this again." Jim began to feel ill. The more he thought about it, the worse he felt. The more he thought about it, the more frightened he became. He knew he had no hope of changing his mother's mind.

The next morning Jim was a wreck. He hardly slept at all and was shaking like a leaf. Upon arriving at the house, they got out of the car and rang the doorbell. Mrs. Thomas opened the door and welcomed them in. Jim could hardly walk, but in he went. Slowly, nervous, and still shaking, Jim walked up to Mr. Thomas and said, "I am so sorry that I did this to you.

I should have never thrown rocks out of the window at cars."

Mr. and Mrs. Thomas looked at each other, then at Jim, and then once again at each other. Mr. Thomas spoke first. "What you did yesterday was truly dangerous. Luckily there was no serious damage and no one got hurt. But what you've done today is truly remarkable. It took a lot of courage to come here and apologize. I wish more adults would do what you did!" Mrs. Thomas added, "Thank you for being so responsible. I am really impressed by what you have done." Jim then offered to pay for the damages that did occur, but Mr. Thomas would have none of that. "The fact that you came here, the fact that you respected us enough to offer an apology, is greater than anything money can buy." Jim was amazed and thankful.

Sarah told me that Jim learned quite a lesson that day. He never forgot that experience and brought it up several times in later years. For example, when someone would do something wrong at school, Jim would come home and talk to Sarah about it. He would say, "Hey mom, remember when you took me to apologize to Mr. Thomas? I will never forget that. It reminds me to do the right thing, no matter how hard it seems to do."

Recently I spoke again with Sarah and reminded her about this story. She had an interesting addendum. It turns out that the reason that Sarah did what she did was that she remembered a story that her father told her. When he was a young boy on the west side of Chicago, he went into a grocery store and stole a candy bar. He brought it home and was eating it when his mother asked him where he got it. He told her the truth. His mother made him go back and face the owner of the store, pay him for the candy bar, and apologize. Her father told her how humiliating that was, but also how important it was. Sarah never forgot that story. Her father's moment of encounter became part of her "genetic makeup" and expressed itself when Jim faced a similar moment of encounter.

We can see the principle that in life we can either win or we learn from these examples of moments of encounter. As we encounter the moments in our life and business, we are often faced with significant problems. These problems include:

*   Experiencing difficulty in relationships with employees and customers;
*   feeling unsuccessful from a lack of profitability, unmet goals, or from a sense of disconnection from meaning and purpose;
*   experiencing a lack of control over employees and customers; our work seems to control us.
*   suffering from overwork affects our personal life.

Even when things are going well, life throws us curve balls such as illnesses, accidents, family troubles, death, and natural disasters. These problems are related to unmet expectations. We feel that we have lost. This leads to stress, suffering, and pain causing us to cry out "Why me?"

In moments of encounter one can choose to lose or to learn. You can learn how to tap into your spiritual intelligence, your wisdom, and your soul, and thereby improve your thinking and/or your acting in your business and your life. Through better thinking you can understand both the source of your problems and find ways of fixing them. Through better acting you can engage in better service to customers and your team. Thinking and acting on purpose in moments of encounter leads to a life with much more joy and inner peace, much more happiness—shalom.

The Miracle in the Moment

Hidden within each moment of encounter, hidden in the problems and issues at work and at home, is the potential to transform the ordinary world by infusing it with Holiness. By connecting to the metaphysical Light hidden yet present in any moment of encounter, you can find your path to happiness.

Awareness of the metaphysical dimension in any moment of encounter opens you to the potential for there to be a miracle in any moment. What do I mean when I use the term miracle?

Many of us have heard the story before (Exodus:14). The children of Israel left Egypt and Moses led them into the wilderness. They arrive at the sea with the Egyptians chasing after them and surrounding them from the rear. Water this way, Egyptians that way, what were they going to do? What happened? A miracle! God split the sea and the children of Israel walked through the sea to freedom. How nice, how convenient, how incredible!

The question, of course, is was that natural or supernatural? What does it mean for there to be a miracle? Was there a spontaneous cessation of the laws of nature? Was this the "real" God showing up, active and powerful? Several times in the story the Bible points out that the children of Israel walked in the "dryness" in the midst of the sea (wetness). Notice the paradox. This event is a moment filled with paradox. Was this moment natural or supernatural? Yes! Was this the laws of science, the laws of nature, in action or was this God acting? Yes! At a certain level both are true. It's up to us to decide which we will take to be true.

What is a miracle? The Random House dictionary defines a miracle as:

1. An effect or extraordinary event in the physical world that surpasses all known human or natural powers and is ascribed to a supernatural cause.
2. Such an effect or event manifesting or considered as a work of God.
3. A wonder; marvel.

It is derived from the Latin meaning to wonder at.

Notice the three characteristics: a wondrous event, of supernatural cause, and a work of God. One can have a wondrous event that can be explained by natural causes. That would seem to rule out its being miraculous. One can have a wondrous event without bringing God into the picture. Science restricts itself to the concept that all explanations of cause must be contained within nature, within the space-time box itself. There is no such thing as a supernatural cause. One cannot rely on God to explain events and observations. Science definitionally eliminates miracles. That is scientific faith, a scientific assumption. When asked, "How do you know this?" The scientist says, "I have no need for miracles. Just because I can't explain it naturally today does not mean I will never be able to explain it using only natural causation." Please notice this is a paradigm, a possibly correct interpretation. However, it is possibly incorrect.

Let me share with you the traditional Jewish view regarding miracles. First of all, the Hebrew word for miracle is 'nase' (pronounced with a long "a" sound and a silent "E"). The root of the word has three meanings: trial, miracle, and banner. This leads to three parts to any miracle.

A miracle is first of all a *trial*—a test. It is a challenge—a moment of encounter. At work or at home we run into difficulties, we come across problems, and we have skirmishes and clashes with others. Not only are these confrontations problematic in themselves, but the deeper challenge is can we see God involved in these events even though he is hidden?

Secondly, a *miracle* is a low probability event with a *possible "natural" explanation and appearance.* The wondrous and amazing part of a miracle is the timing and God's involvement. Our job is to perceive the miracles in this world. We have to ask ourselves if we can take a spiritual approach (awareness of the presence of the metaphysical within our physical world) to this moment. Can we re-meta-member? We need to be looking for messengers with messages.

Third, upon experiencing a miracle we must raise a *banner.* We need to show gratitude for the miracle in any moment and publicize our appreciation using *banner* headlines.

This goes deeply into the Jewish understanding of the universe. What is nature? The root of the Hebrew word for nature is "seal." Nature is the seal of God and is a creation of God. The world operates naturally. Remember, God has withdrawn to create this world. God operates in this world hidden behind the laws of nature. God is not in nature, but is above it, thus transcending it. God created this world with His wisdom; therefore nature is, in theory, understandable. God makes science possible.

However, God is not only interested in nature. God is not only the **Power** Greater Than Ourselves; He is also the **Loving** greater Than Ourselves. God is far more interested in human beings and relationships than in the cosmos. God created nature, but he also created human beings. He placed within us a consciousness (mind-wisdom) and gave us a conscience (soul) that empowers us to rise beyond the natural world and create a human world of relationships.

More than nature, God is interested in history. There is his-story (small h) the story of man and there is His-story (large H) the story of God. Judaism believes that we write those stories together in covenant. We have freedom, responsibility, and purpose, all of which are gifts from God. How we choose to use those gifts is our responsibility—our ability to respond to the call of God.

A miracle (nase) is first of all then a test, a trial, and a challenge. The challenge is whether or not we can see God even when he is hidden. Can we see the miracles in our life? Can we see God's messengers in those events with messages that can change our lives? Can we climb Jacob's ladder? Can we learn the lessons from the Ladder of Learning? Because God has withdrawn, even the most miraculous of events and most wondrous of occurrences can appear to be completely natural. God is in this place but I, I did not know. I need to pay attention. I can choose to hear the voice or not. For us to have free choice, God must be hidden.

Notice the biblical text itself, "then Moses stretched out his hand over the sea, and all that night the Lord drove the sea back with a strong east wind and he turned it into dry land." (Exodus 14: 21) It seems that the Bible is claiming a natural explanation for one of its most famous supernatural events. In Judaism, a miracle is not necessarily something that suspends natural law. It is an event whose timing and characteristics evoke amazement and wonder.

We must work at seeing the hidden hand of God in our universe. We must learn to see God's miracles and messengers in our everyday lives. Remember, the uncertainty contributes to our free will. We are God's eyes and ears, we are God's witnesses, and we are His partners here on Earth. Our job is to find God, who is hidden beneath the challenges, trials, and tribulations, in a moment of encounter. We need to connect to that hidden presence and to bring God and his timeless values back into this world.

A moment of encounter can become a moment of holiness where we transform an ordinary moment into a miraculous, wondrous, and extraordinary moment. We are to raise God's banner. Raising God's banner means to have gratitude for all that God brings us, and publicize that goodness.

Gratitude

A blind man was begging in a city park. Someone approached and asked him whether people were giving generously. The blind man shook a nearly empty tin.

His visitor said to him, "Let me write something on your card." The blind man agreed. That evening the visitor returned and asked, "Well, how were things today?"

The blind and showed him a tin full money and asked, "What on earth did you write on that card?"
"Oh," said the other, "I merely wrote 'Today is a spring day and I am blind.'"[80]

Mordechai Kaplan notes, "it is necessary that, in addition to making ourselves sensitive to what it is that we lack, we cultivate sensitivity to what it is that we have."[81] The visitor was able to sensitize people passing the blind man not only to what the blind man was lacking, but to the blessing and goodness possessed by each passerby.

The essence of religion is the affirmation that life is worthwhile. Belief in God is belief in a power that lovingly assures the possibility of experiencing life as being worth living. When we are gratefully appreciative of the good in life, we are experiencing the reality of God and communing with him. If we want this confidence in the happy possibilities of life to stay with us in any crisis, it is important that we cultivate a spirit of thanksgiving in normal times. We need to practice gratitude every single day. In addition to accustoming ourselves to see, and gratefully enjoy, the good in the daily routine of life, we should habituate ourselves to discovering opportunities for life enhancing experiences as they present themselves to us, and take full advantage of them. We must pay attention to potential moments of encounter.

Robert Emmons in his book, *Thanks*, points out that gratitude "is the acknowledgment of goodness in one's life."[82] It is more than a feeling. Rather, it is a conscious awareness and a form of re-meta-membering. Gratitude is recognizing that the source of this goodness lies at least partially outside of you. It is directed toward others. Expressions of gratitude bind people together in relationships of reciprocity, making them the building blocks of any civil society.

Gratitude supplies life with meaning by seeing life itself as a gift (remember Brian Tracy in chapter 4). It is a key to happiness and a choice we make to see the blessings instead of the curses in any moment of life. Our internal reactions need not be determined by external forces. We can be thankful rather than blame and complain.

Gratitude is the ability to say "**Thank You**". Both words are important here:

* **Thank** is the acknowledgment of goodness in one's life. Even negative things can have positive aspects. It is a conscious choice we make.
* **You** recognizes that the source of this goodness lies outside of you. It acknowledges and appreciates others.

Hope is gratitude expressed for the future. **Hope is seeing a path to a better future with honesty about present problems.** Hope is the ability to see God's messengers all around you and ready to help you if needed. Gratitude and hope lead to inner peace. One can have gratitude in even trying times. Transforming problems into prosperity requires that, no matter what happens, existence itself is seen as a gift. Gratitude becomes a value—an approach toward life.

In moments of encounter the most important other is the Power and Loving Greater Than Ourselves, God. Emmons points out that wherever there is religion, there is gratitude. Studies have shown that people who described themselves as either religious or spiritual are more likely to be grateful than those who describe themselves as neither. "For a person who has religious or spiritual beliefs, gratitude sets up a relationship to the Divine, to the source from which all good comes. It is a relationship that recognizes the gift of life from the Creator. Choosing to live in that space of recognition repositioned one into a heavenly sphere of humility, awe, and recognition of how blessed one is to have the opportunity to learn, grow, love, create share, and help others ….Grateful people sense that they are not separate from others or from God. This recognition itself brings a deep of gratefulness."[83] Emmons' "space of recognition" is what Covey calls "the space between stimulus and response" and what I call "a moment of encounter." Gratitude is the final step of any successful moment of encounter.

Emmons interviewed a woman with post-polio syndrome. Here is her story:

"One of my most profound experiences of thankfulness came at the birth of my first child. I had wondered, all my growing up years, as to whether I would be able to have children, whether I could care for children with only one arm, and whether God would choose to bless me in that way. When my daughter was born, all the nursing staff showed distrust of my ability as a caretaker. However, I realized that God had chosen to bless me with a child, and he would bless me with physical needs to care for her. Since God had not chosen to spare me from polio, I knew my having a baby was no sure thing. Therefore, when she was born, I praised God for allowing my husband and me to share the joy of molding a new human being into a blessing to God. We were excited about the magnitude of our job, and I felt expectant and hopeful. What greater purpose could I ever have than to raise another human? None, and that was the joy in my thankfulness—the joy of meaning and purpose in life."[84]

For this woman, thankfulness and gratitude lead to joy, meaning, and purpose—happiness.

Emmons quotes Kenneth Pargament who described the power of religion to transform the meaning of events in this way: "When the sacred is seen working its will in life's events, what first seems random, nonsensical, and tragic is changed into something else—an opportunity to appreciate life more fully, a chance to be with God, a challenge to help others grow, or a loving act meant to prevent something worse from taking place."[85] It is in these times of greatest stress, in searching for meaning the religion seems to exert its greatest influence.

Wayne Dyer in his book, *Manifest Your Destiny*, notes the connection between gratitude and wholeness. When you are filled with gratitude, you cannot feel alienated or separate. Gratitude is an expression of love in the form of a thank you to God for the gift of life. It empowers us to feel more connected and therefore more whole. Gratitude offers powerful healing. When you are filled with gratitude, when you are grateful for everything, you cannot focus on what is missing, you cannot be a victim, you are no longer broken, and you are healed.

Dyer points out 3 obstacles to gratitude.[86]
1. *Finding fault*: This focuses on what is missing rather than on being grateful for what you have.
2. *Complaining*: One who complains feels deprived,

isolated, and separated from goodness and joyfulness. This leads to ingratitude. The solution is to stop complaining and explaining.

3. *Taking what you have for granted*: Every experience can be a moment of encounter with a significant other. We can fail to appreciate those close to us and the gifts from God until it's too late and they are gone.

Dyer also lists several facilitators to gratitude.[87]

1. Develop an awareness of yourself as a recipient rather than as a victim.
2. Tell those around you how much you appreciate them.
3. Avoid explaining and complaining as much as possible.
4. Begin and end each day with an expression of gratitude and thanksgiving.
5. Be grateful for the suffering and struggles that are a part of the fabric of your life.

The last facilitator, being grateful for the suffering and struggles that are part of the fabric of your life, brings us full circle. We began our journey in this book with the question "Why me?" Why do I suffer with pain and problems? We noted that problems are the flipside of purpose. If there were no problems in this world, none of us would be able to act on purpose. The power of purpose overrides the pain of problems. Therefore, I would add one more facilitator:

6. Be grateful for your purpose, your "So That___!

Have gratitude for your ability to think and act on purpose and for the healing power of timeless values, especially the four healing values: Light, Love, Life, & ShaLom.

The paradox that we have discovered in this journey is that the answer to our initial question of why do we suffer with pain and problems is actually so that we can be grateful for that pain and those problems! Moments of encounter are instants of challenge and trial, testing whether we can see the blessing, opportunity, and even miracles present in the pain and problems themselves. Can we be grateful for those moments, for those problems? Einstein was right. We cannot solve our problems at the same level of thinking we were at when we created them. Instead of being a victim with pain and problems in moments of encounter, we can choose to be victors and have gratitude for our pain and problems, and this empowers us to solve our pain and problems.

In any moment of encounter we can begin to solve our problems through the three values from the lessons of learning. We must use our *freedom* in that moment of challenge to pause and choose *responsibility*. Our responsibility is to think (re-meta-member) and act (loving acts of service) on our unique *purpose*. While freedom, responsibility, and purpose help us focus on the moment of encounter *inside* the space-time box, the four healing values (Light, Love, Life, and ShaLom) empower us to connect to the spiritual/metaphysical aspect of any moment of encounter *outside* the space-time box. In any moment of encounter, we can reattach to our purpose using the four healing values. Through Light we can make the Timeless Values Connection in the metaphysical realm, reaffirming our purpose. That purpose will be some unique form of Love, of extending yourself and taking action to serve others. The power of that purpose overrides the pain of problems. We are thus empowered to return into the space-time box, to return into our Life. Back at work, back at home, we act on that purpose, solving problems and healing pain.

Life is a journey through moments of encounter along your path to happiness. We exit the moment of encounter by taking action in some way, expressing our gratitude, and then living with the consequences of that action. If our thinking and acting were successful, if we connected to proper spiritual truth, brought that truth into our lives at work and at home, and through acting on that truth transformed this world into an extraordinary, holy, place then we are open to the possibility of God granting shalom—Happiness.

Happiness, then, is only possible when we have gratitude. Remarkably, it applies especially to being grateful for the suffering and struggles that are part of the fabric of your life. Upon receiving the Nobel Peace Prize, Holocaust survivor and author Elie Wiesel had this to say about gratitude:

"No one is as capable of gratitude as one who has emerged from the Kingdom of night. We know that every moment is a moment of grace, every hour an offering; not to share them would mean to betray them. Our lives no longer belong to us alone; they belong to all those who need us desperately...And that is why I swore never to be silent whenever and wherever human beings endure suffering and humiliation. We must always take sides. Neutrality helps the oppressor, never the victim. Silence encourages the tormentor, never the tormented."[88]

We must tell our story. We must share our experiences in life's journey through moments of encounter.

Path Principles

* Responsibility is the name of the human game.
* Responsibility is the ability to accept what is and choose a response that is extraordinary in any moment of encounter.
* A moment of encounter is an instant of engagement with the past, present, and future in which we can choose to transform our lives from ordinary to extraordinary (become holy).
* A moment of encounter is an opportunity to engage the spiritual potential present in our physical space-time universe.
* In any moment of encounter we can choose to be happy, choose our path to happiness, and experience moments of happiness.
* A miracle is:
    * First of all a *trial*—a test. It is a challenge—a moment of encounter.
    * Secondly, a *miracle* is a low probability event with a *possible "natural" explanation and appearance.* The wondrous and amazing part of a miracle is the timing and God's involvement.
    * Third, upon experiencing a miracle we must raise a *banner.* We need to show gratitude for the miracle in any moment.

* Hope is gratitude expressed for the future. Gratitude and hope lead to inner peace.
* Gratitude is the ability to say thank you.
* Happiness is only possible when we have gratitude.
* Remarkably, gratitude applies especially to being grateful for the suffering and struggles that are part of the fabric of your life.

— CHAPTER 9: —
SEEK HAPPINESS—SHALOM

Path Prescription #9: Staying on the Mat at Work and at Home

My youngest daughter was a fascinating challenge as a child. She would get angry at school and act out inappropriately. She often got into arguments with her mother and me, getting upset, running into her room, and throwing herself onto her bed. I took it upon myself to follow her into her room. I would ask her permission to be with her and she would usually shrug her shoulders. I would sit on her bed and usually simply wait for her to talk. Occasionally, I would ask if she wanted to talk. Invariably, she would respond with a shrug of her shoulders. In fact, I quickly learned that no matter what question I asked, I always got a shrug of her shoulders. After a while, I found it easier to just come in the room, sit on the bed, and wait for her to start talking. I would sit, and sit, and sit, and often fall asleep on her bed. Whenever I would fall asleep, she would push me until I woke up. I would ask her if she wanted to talk and, shock of all shocks, I would usually get another shrug of her shoulders.

Now, Bill Cosby has said that your children will act this way because they know they will live longer than you, and therefore they will win. In the case of my daughter, however, usually after a while she would talk. I might have to wait over an hour, but eventually she needed to talk. At first, however, she needed to be silent. I believed that it was extremely important that I honor that silence. I knew that there was no silence in her brain, so I sat on her bed waiting for her to work things out to her satisfaction so that she would be ready to talk to me. I wanted her to know that I was there for her and it was up to her to begin a conversation.

Recently, she brought up those experiences. She said to me, "Dad, I just want you to know how important it was to me that you sat with me for all those hours, for all those years. I would not be the person that I am today had you not done that." I asked her, "What about that experience made such a difference to you?" She replied, "First of all, I really did want you to come after me and to sit on my bed, but it was a stage in my life when I could not say that. The fact that you came up without my having to ask you to come after me let me know that you understood what I wanted without my having to suffer through telling you. I ran out of the room because I was upset and I wanted people to know that I was upset. When you came after me, it showed that you knew I was upset. You validated my feelings."

"The method that you used worked quite well. You didn't push stuff out of me. You didn't yell at me, and you had patience. In fact, you had so much patience that often you fell asleep.

But that was okay because you were there, and that was all that mattered to me. In your silent presence you were saying that it is okay that I was upset. When I was ready, which could be hours, I could talk to you about it. At that point you were able to show me that my thinking and/or acting was wrong and that I needed to do something to make it better. You were able to teach me the lessons that I needed to learn. What I appreciated most was that you didn't say, 'If you need to talk I'm here for you,' and then leave. You said, 'If you need to talk to me I'm here,' and stayed. That way I never had to chase after you. I would have never come after you."

"Whenever I got upset about something, I felt isolated, alone, and broken. I certainly did not feel calm, peaceful, complete, filled with happiness and shalom. By your being there, I did not have to deal with that part of the problem. All I had to focus on was the struggle in my head: Say something, don't say something, say something, or don't say something. I didn't have to deal with the issues of why doesn't anybody care enough about me to notice that I am in my room all upset, why doesn't someone come up after me, and why doesn't someone love me."

"When I went upstairs, I took my paradigm, my understanding, of what had just happened with me. When you came into the room and sat on my bed, you validated my understanding. There was the possibility that I was right. It didn't matter whether I was really right or wrong—what mattered was that it was okay to think the way I was thinking. Once I felt that the way I was thinking was okay, then we could deal with the actual right or wrong. Without that validation, I might have never been willing to discuss the possibility that I could have been wrong. That validation enabled me to feel calmer, more accepted, more connected, and more whole—I felt a sense of shalom. As hard as the situation was, I could be at peace with it because there was meaning to it. The meaning was that I felt validated, accepted, and loved. Just feeling heard and being understood gave me the peaceful feeling. Once I had that feeling, I could continue on to finding a solution to the actual problem that caused me to run upstairs in the first place."

"It took me many years to work out my problems. But I could have never worked them out without the start that you gave me."

"Dad," she finished, "I just want to say thank you."

Wow! Talk about joy, inner peace, moments of happiness and shalom! For me, that moment was off the charts! Notice the power of gratitude. Notice how it affects both people involved. For my daughter, saying thank you showed that she had recognized the benefit she had received. In saying thank you she also returned the favor (passing it forward), creating a cycle of grateful loving that now included me. The expression of gratitude between two people leads to a loving connection, harmonic unity, joy, and inner peace. In other words, it leads to happiness and shalom. For me, that moment of happiness was preceded by a process that took years to actualize. Years during which I could never be sure that my message was being heard.

Now I must ask the question, was it worth the wait? It certainly was and for two reasons. First of all, I had achieved happiness. As we have discussed throughout the book, I had traveled along *my* path to happiness, in this case at home. I had actualized one of my primary values, which was to be of service at home for each member of my family. The path I had taken began by searching for Light, for my purpose. I made a Timeless Values Connection and identified being of service at home to be one of my prioritized values.

Next, using that value for this particular daughter, with her particular issues, I realized that an extraordinary way of serving her would be to listen with love and teach her *"Your Path to Happiness."* This completed the process of *thinking on purpose*. It was now my responsibility to *act on purpose*, act with Love, at my next opportunity. My daughter was quite cooperative at this stage supplying me with many moments of encounter, moments in my Life where she tested and challenged me, to act in alignment with my values and purpose. By following her to her room and by listening to her on her bed, I had to extend myself for the purpose of nurturing her spiritual growth, in other words, Love her.

So far I had traveled along my path to happiness using the values Light, Love, and Life. What about ShaLom? What about joy and inner peace—happiness? When my daughter said, "Thank you," I had a moment of extreme happiness. She validated me in my assessment that I had actualized my purpose as a father. I felt balanced harmonious unity and wholeness in actualizing that value. I had joy and inner peace, happiness—shaLom.

But what about all those years sitting on the bed? Here is the second reason that it was worth the wait. Life is not only about the destination, it is far more about the journey to the destination. It is *your path to happiness,* not simply *achieving* happiness. You can choose to be happy while on your path to happiness. George Leonard in his book, *Mastery,* speaks of the journey of mastery not so much as a goal or a destination but rather a long term process—a journey. The focus of American culture currently is on the opposite concept. It focuses on the climactic moment. Watch any current TV commercial and you will probably see an example of this. People might be working at a job for a few moments, and then it's party time and out comes the beer! Life at its best, these commercials teach, is an endless series of climactic moments. One fantasy is crowded out by the next. There is no plateau.

Leonard points out, "How do you best move toward mastery? To put it simply, you practice diligently, but you practice primarily *for the sake of the practice itself.* Rather than being frustrated while on the plateau, you learn to appreciate and enjoy it just as much as you do the upward surges."[89]

To become a master in any endeavor requires practice. Even more important than practice as some action that you *do*, is practice as something that you *have*, or something that you *are*. As a dentist I practiced dentistry, but I also had a dental "practice." If that practice is only a collection of patients, or a way of making a living, it is an ordinary practice. It is not a master's practice. For an extraordinary practice, a master's practice, rewards gained along the way are okay, but they are not the main reason for the journey. The journey is for its own sake. Masters love to practice. Because they practice, they develop good habits. They get better and better enjoying what they do more and more. They love the plateau.

"Practice, the path of mastery, exists only in the present. You can see it, hear it, smell it, feel it. To love the plateau is to love the eternal now, to enjoy the inevitable spurts of progress in the fruits of accomplishment, then serenely to accept the new plateau that waits just beyond them."[90]

"What is mastery? At the heart of it, mastery is practice. Mastery is staying on the path...[91] **The master is the one who stays on the mat five minutes longer every day than anybody else."[92]**

Your path to happiness at work and at home requires you to have a "practice" at both work and at home. You must look for mastery in both places. You must learn to practice—to stay on the mat. In the case of my daughter, I needed to stay on the bed. Staying on the bed itself made me happy. Every moment on the bed was a moment of loving my daughter. Paying attention to the value I was adding to her life made me happy. Integrating my behaviors with the power of my purpose enabled me to overcome the problems of the length of the process. By enjoying staying on the bed (staying on the mat) I often experienced joy and inner peace, happiness and shaLom along the way.

This was not the same level of joyful inner peace and happiness that one receives at a climactic peak moment in life (for example when my daughter said thank you). Being happy along the path requires that the journey itself needs to be rewarding. For this to happen, you must think and act on purpose whenever you are on life's mat. The power of that purpose overrides the pain of staying on the mat. In fact, it empowers you to choose to be happy while you are on the mat every day at work and at home. Purpose gives you a reason to be happy at every moment along your path. Recall Brian Tracy's words, "Happiness has been defined as the progressive realization of a worthy ideal. You can only be happy as long as you're working step by step toward something that is really important to you."

Being happy comes from realizing short term inner peace—shalom. Achieving happiness is a long term choice. Part of the secret of realizing short term inner peace requires connecting to timeless values, especially the timeless values most important to you. That requires thinking on purpose. Once you have identified your purpose and your primary values, then you must act on purpose. Those values must be reflected in what you do in your life *every day* at work and at home. Thinking and acting on purpose, choosing to connect what is important to you with what you do each day, leads to the joy and inner peace that each of us seeks from life. Inner peace, shalom, heals us from life's pain and problems. Happy is what you choose to be.

Happiness is what you choose to become. Eventually, to have long term joy and inner peace—to achieve shalom—you must focus on others as well as yourself. You must focus on being of service. You must find a practice that HEALS others. You must find a practice that **H**elps **E**mpower **A**cts of **L**oving **S**ervice. You must find a practice that helps others experience joy and inner peace. To achieve that SHALOM, you must use the healing power of timeless values to help:

        Solve problems
        Heal pain
        Address needs
        Look to satisfy wants
        Overcome challenges
        Make opportunities

AT WORK
&
AT HOME

Regarding my daughter, I helped her **S**olve some of her problems by active listening and by teaching her how to do problem-solving once she felt heard. I helped **H**eal her pain by following her up to her bedroom, sitting on her bed, letting her know that I was available to help, and showing her that I loved her regardless of her behavior. This in no way meant that I approved of her behavior, and she understood that fact. I helped **A**ddress her needs for feeling validated, loved, and free to express her feelings openly. Most importantly here, I gave her the space and the time necessary for her to be able and ready to work out her problems. I **L**ooked for ways to satisfy her wants, such as:

* wanting to talk to someone, but not being ready to talk—I waited;
* she wanted my attention—I came into her bedroom and sat with her;
* she wanted to solve her problem—eventually I was able to actively listen to her.

I helped her learn to **O**vercome challenges by coming to her room, sitting on her bed, waiting for her to speak, and offering my suggestions once she asked for help. These actions made her feel respected and validated. I also showed her that I believed she could overcome challenges if she wanted to, and then showed her how. Finally, I believe that all these actions together empowered my daughter by **M**aking an opportunity for her to model my behavior for herself and others in the future.

She ran up the stairs to her room with a problem that existed only because of the way she was thinking. My ability to go up there and change her paradigm relied on me simply being there at first. The worst thing that I could do at first was to tell her my paradigm of what I had just seen. That's why active listening is essential in any loving relationship, in trying to resolve problems peacefully and to have shalom. In mentoring that behavior, I was making an opportunity for my daughter to learn the power of active listening.

Focusing on my key values, I was able to be happy in the short term and achieve happiness in the long term. Thus, in both the short and long term, I experienced shalom at work and at home.

What about this experience from the perspective of my daughter? Was it worth the wait?

In the long term, she clearly thought it was worth the wait. She had gratitude and expressed that gratitude by saying thank you to me. I happen to know she also has gratitude to the Power and Loving Greater Than Ourselves. She turned out to be a very spiritual woman. She is a woman of deep faith, but she did not come upon that faith easily. Hers was a long and difficult struggle. She spent many years on the mat. She continues on that mat today, and she is still struggling with being happy while on the mat.

Essentially, the act of running up to her room in anger was the equivalent at her age of asking the question with which this book began, **"Why me?"** She was asking, "Why do I suffer from problems and pain? In the presence of life's challenges, how can I achieve happiness?"

I taught her, as I hope I have you, that there is a path to happiness at work and at home. **Path Prescriptions** and tools for negotiating this path successfully do exist. While speaking to her on her bed, I introduced her to each of the path prescriptions.

Primary Path Prescription: Using Timeless Values for Thinking and Acting on Purpose

Path Prescriptions for Thinking on Purpose:

Path Prescription #2: The Lessons of Learning

Path Prescription #3: The Universal Whole-Parts-Whole Process

Path Prescription #4: Thinking about Happiness—Setting Proper Expectations

Path Prescription #5: Knowing 101—The Ladder of Learning

Path Prescriptions for Acting on Purpose:

Path Prescription #6: The Timeless Values Connection (**Light**)

Path Prescription #7: The Sacred Path of Serving Others (**Love**)

Path Prescription #8: Moments of Encounter (Life)

Path Prescription #9: Staying on the Mat at Work and at Home (Happiness & ShaLom)

Using the path prescriptions she learned the following:

In trying to answer the question, **"Why me?"** I taught her that there are three lessons of learning:

1. "Why me?" I will never know for sure. Absolute truth exists but I will never know it absolutely. There is uncertainty from both science and spirituality (faith), and that can lead to mistakes. But just that very uncertainty leads to my **freedom** to choose my response in any situation.

2. "Why me?" I want to know anyway. To be perfectly human is to know imperfectly. **Responsibility** is searching for truth and doing the right thing in the presence of uncertainty.

3. "Why me?" What is it that I want to know? I want to know my **purpose**.

She could be a victor instead of a victim. My daughter started as a victim. As a victim her answer to the question, "Why me?" was "Because ____." and she would fill that blank with blame for somebody or something else controlling her life. She struck out at those whom she blamed. Over time, staying on the bed, she learned to change the question from "Why me, why do I suffer from pain and problems?" to "Why me?

Why do I exist?" Her new answer to "Why me?" became "So That___!" Over time, she filled that blank with her unique purpose and her most important values. Over time, she felt less the victim and celebrated more success becoming a victor. She learned to use the power of her purpose to override the pain of any of her problems.

She learned that the source of pain and problems can be found in the universal whole-parts-whole process. She identified those things that made her feel broken into parts and those things that made her feel more whole. She began to understand that being separated from God through creation and our birth leads us to a state of imbalance, disharmony, and lack of wholeness. She learned that she needed to move from parts back to whole. I taught her that the process of moving from parts to whole is what I call *Your Path to Happiness*. I reviewed with her the use of the four healing values, Light, Love, Life, & ShaLom, to overcome life's imbalance, disharmony, and brokenness and achieve joy and inner peace—happiness.

She learned that happy is what she chooses to be, while happiness is what she chooses to become. Her challenge was to be happy while becoming someone who achieves happiness. Being happy is something that she can realize at any time, while happiness is something achieved over time. Happiness is the whole that emerges from a life well lived—a life lived on purpose.

She learned that spirituality is an awareness of the existence of a higher dimension. Spirituality is the notion that there is more than simply a physical universe—more than just our space-time box. While inside the space-time box, science can answer questions of *how* things work and *what* is going on in our world, but it cannot tell us about the metaphysical—that which comes from outside the space-time box.

Science cannot answer deep "Why" questions. It can tell us what, but it cannot tell us what for; it can tell us how but not why. It cannot tell us about values meaning or purpose. We need spirituality to learn timeless values, objective meaning, and ultimate purpose. Using science and religion, as well as the rest of the Mosaic of Knowledge, as well as the Ladder of Learning, gave my daughter a greater understanding of the universe as a whole, not just its parts.

My daughter learned how to use the four healing values, Light, Love, Life, & ShaLom. First she learned how to search for Light. She learned how to make the timeless values connection using Light as the source of purpose, as the source of timeless values. She is still learning her unique purpose. She has moved on to Love, being of service. She recently got married and is learning about the Sacred Path of Serving Others and its virtues. She is learning to have covenantal, as opposed to contractual, relationships with others. Each day she learns more about Life, the ordered spiritual growth that comes from actualizing her potential. She is looking for a vocation and has experienced many moments of encounter. Finally, through this process, along her journey, at times she has experienced ShaLom. She has been healing, becoming more balanced, in greater harmony with herself and with others. She has enjoyed more inner peace, happiness, than she did in the past.

Inner peace comes from integrity, from keeping your behavior—what you do every day in your life—in harmony and integrated with your highest values. The more your values are in harmony with timeless values, God's values, you will experience more happiness and shalom through the days of your life.

I am very confident that she will pass this gift, *Your Path to Happiness*, on to her children and her children to their children. It's not up to any of us to finish the job, but we are all responsible to partake in some of the work. We must engage everyone in the process, even though while we are alive we will never finally arrive.

The rabbis of the Talmud took note of this life as a process. Rabbi Abin the Levite said, "When a man takes leave of his fellow, he should not say to him 'go in peace', but rather 'go to peace'…One who takes leave of the dead should not say to him 'go to peace', but 'go in peace.'"[93]

The world in which we live, our space-time box, is a world of process and a world of change. We are always becoming. Our goal in life should be to journey on a path of constant improvement, learning, and growth. We are subject to the whole-parts-whole universal process. Before creation or our birth we were whole. In that preexistence, we experienced shalom—balanced harmonious unity.

By creating the universe, God withdrew, leaving behind our space-time box, a universe of parts. At birth, we enter this broken world and we become parts, separated from God. We would like to reconnect to God. We wish that would be easy. We would like to arrive at total and permanent joy and inner peace (happiness and shalom). We would like to be able to go through our life *in peace*. However, while we are alive we never finally arrive. Entropy, the random disorder in nature, in the space time box, takes over. After reaching a peak, we always go back on the plateau. We live most of life on the mat. While in this world we never experience being *in peace* permanently. We do experience moments of peace, a few peak experiences, as part of the process. In our quest for peace, we go <u>to</u> *peace*. Life is *Your Path <u>to</u> Happiness.*

This is the message of Rabbi Abin. Only in the afterlife, after death, do we experience permanent peace. It is only in the metaphysical that is there no change, only the eternal present. Therefore, if one is at a cemetery visiting a loved one, upon leaving one says, "Go *in peace*." This is similar to saying, "May you rest in peace." However, when one takes leave of another living human being one offers the blessing, "May you *go to peace*."

The Jewish concept of an afterlife is not the world *to* come. It is the world *that* comes. How you act here in this world affects and becomes what you experience in the next world. In this world we can choose to head <u>to</u> peace. If we do that, then in the next world we exist <u>in</u> peace.

Can we experience more inner peace in this world while on our path to permanent peace? I believe we can by choosing to be happy while on life's mat. Remember, happy is what you choose to be and happiness is what you choose to become. I believe that the experience of being on the mat in and of itself can bring a sense of balance, harmony, and wholeness into your world. Enjoying staying on the mat transforms a potentially undesirable negative experience (practice) into a positive experience. By thinking and acting on purpose, focusing on the long term benefits of practicing something that you enjoy, that you do well, that others value, that you value, and is in alignment with timeless values, you will achieve more moments of peace, wholeness, and shalom along your path to happiness at work and at home in this world.

Our path through life can be viewed as a quest that requires practice. Life is difficult. Life is a terminal condition. We cannot cure this condition, but through practice we can heal. Through practicing using the healing power of values, especially Light, Love, Life, & ShaLom we can achieve victory in our vocation—our "practice." For me, it started as the practice of dentistry and now it is the practice of writing and the practice of speaking. For you, it might be the practice of parenting, the practice of your religion, the practice of your profession, or maybe just the practice of being you. Life is a path—a process. It is a sacred path of serving others. It is *Your Path to Happiness.*

There will be times when we will fall off of the path. There are times when we will be off the mat. Expect to experience problems, failures, obstacles, and setbacks. Our responsibility is to reconnect with the Power and Loving Greater Than Ourselves. We must get back on the mat, return to the path, and reconnect with thinking and acting on purpose. As Rob Stearns pointed out, "You lose because you're human, but you win because you are you." All humans experience problems and loss in their lives. But only you can find your unique way to overcome your challenges—to win or to learn!

So, in the end this is our answer to the three purpose questions that we asked in the introduction.

Q1 is: Why do we suffer from problems?
Pain and problems exist <u>so that</u> we can heal that pain and solve those problems.

Our purpose is to solve our own, as well as each other's, problems leading to joy and inner peace—happiness. Without problems we would have no purpose. Purpose is the flipside of problems. We can focus on purpose or problems. If we focus on problems, we will have pain; if we focus on purpose then:

The power of purpose overrides the pain of problems!

*Q2 is: What is our general, **human**, purpose here? Why do we exist?*

We exist <u>so that</u> we can love others. We love others through action—not through feelings. Life is a sacred path of serving others. In being of service and solving problems for others, we fulfill our general human purpose, which is to love and to serve at work and at home.

*Q3 is: What is our specific, **personal**, purpose here? Why are we in business?*

We are in business <u>so that</u> we can solve particular problems for particular individuals. While our general life purpose is to serve others by solving their problems, our business purpose is more specific. We must discover a USP. Your USP is your **Unique Solution** to your customer's **Problem**. We must answer three questions:

1. What is the problem that we solve?
2. What is our systematic solution to that problem?
3. What makes us unique and different from other businesses?

As we go through life trying to fulfill these purposes, we create and live our story. Much of our suffering and problems come from false expectations. We do not necessarily expect life to be difficult and we do not expect to have problems and pain. Healing from this condition requires better thinking. Better thinking helps you to have more appropriate expectations and to get back on the mat more quickly.

In life we either win or we learn. If we learn we hardly ever lose.

You lose because you're human. We will forever make mistakes and we will never understand the answer to all questions perfectly. We will fall off the path—off the mat.
You win because you are you. You have a unique purpose here. You are able to solve specific problems that nobody else can. Because of your unique talents and your unique purpose, you add special value to this world. By connecting to others and being of service to yourself and to others, you either win or you learn along your path in life.

Parkinson's disease has been a blessing in disguise for me. Suffering and problems focus your attention. You must pay attention in order to recognize messengers with messages for you regarding solutions to your problems and helping you discover your purpose in life. You must express gratitude for that help. I love speaking and I love writing. Without the Parkinson's disease or the bike accident, I might have never realized just how important and special these experiences are to me. I might have ended up finishing my days here on earth with some of my music still in me.

No matter what your circumstances are, or how painful and difficult they are, you are completely free to choose your response to those conditions. Using the three lessons of learning—freedom, responsibility, and purpose—choose a response that is extraordinary. Choose to live on purpose using the primary prescription of thinking and acting on purpose. Take responsibility. Search for truth and do the right thing. Stay on purpose as you travel along *Your Path to Happiness*.

Our purpose is to love, to take the broken parts of this universe and put them back together again. We are God's partners in the business of transforming this world from what it is, a world filled with suffering pain and problems, into a world that ought to be, a world filled with success, joy, and inner peace.

I want to bless you with shalom—with peace. Shalom is balanced, harmonious unity—a state of wholeness. Balanced refers to healing. A state of health and wholeness is a state of balance. Harmonious refers to the different parts working together. Each individual is unique. When creating a team or working together with others, harmonious unity emerges from the uniqueness of each part and of each person working together with others. That unity is not uniformity. We must value differences to get Harmony. We can be unified around one primary value and we can be unified through one special meaning and purpose. Shalom is the integrated whole that requires integrity. Our job is to take the parts and seek to unify them by connecting everything to the Power and Loving Greater Than Ourselves—to God.

Each one of us is a valuable part of the yet to be connected whole. Each of us has an **extraordinary purpose** for which we were put here and has a responsibility to discover that purpose. Each of us can then play our unique part in the universal symphony. If we include in that symphony the power and loving, which comes from the Power and Loving Greater Than Ourselves, **there is no limit to the problems we can solve, to the healing we can bring, or to the extraordinary harmony that we can create.**

> *A Sufi story sums it up nicely:*
> *Past the seeker, as he prayed, came the crippled, and the beggar, and the beaten. And seeing them, the holy one went down into deep prayer and cried, "Great God how is it that a loving Creator can see such things and yet do nothing about them?"*
>
> *And out of the long silence came God's extraordinary answer, "I did do something about them. I made you."*[94]

Shalom!

—APPENDIX—

The following two lists are to be used as directed in Chapter 6.

LIST OF POSSIBLE CHOICES OF VALUES

Accomplishment

Adventure

Beauty

Boldness

Candor

Challenges

Character

Cheerfulness

Clarity

Cleverness

Collaboration

Commitment

Communication

Community

Compassion

Competition

Control

Cooperation

Courage

Creativity

Dependability

Discipline

Ecology

Efficiency

Environmentalism

Equality

Excellence

Excitement

Fairness

Faith

Family

Financial Security

Flexibility

Forgiveness

Freedom

Friendship

Fulfillment

Fullness

Fun

Generosity

Gratitude	Originality
Growth	Patience
Happiness	Peace
Happy	Persistence
Harmony	Perspective
Health	Potential
Holiness	Power
Honesty	Power & Loving Greater Than
Honor	Ourselves
Humor	Practice
Independence	Principles
Influence	Productivity
Initiative	Profitability
Innovation	Prosperity
Integrity	Prudence
Interdependence	Purpose
Justice	Quality
Kindness	Recognition
Leadership	Recreation
Learning	Relationship
Liberty	Religion
Life	Reputation
Light	Resources
Love	Respect
Loyalty	Responsibility
Nature	Responsiveness
Obedience	Security
Order	Self-Respect

Service

Shalom

Sincerity

Spirituality

Spirituality/Religion

Spouse

Stewardship

Strength

Success

Supp

Teamwork

Time

Timeless Values

Tradition

Trust

Trustworthy

Truth

Wealth

Wisdom

Work

POSSIBLE ADDITIONAL CHOICES OF VERBS
(A) FOR YOUR PURPOSE STATEMENT:

Accomplish acquire adopt advance affect affirm alleviate amplify appreciate ascend associate believe bestow brighten build call cause choose claim collect combine command communicate compel compete complete compliment compose conceive confirm connect consider construct contact continue counsel create decide defend delight deliver demonstrate devise direct discover discuss distribute draft dream drive educate elect embrace encourage endow engage engineer enhance enlighten enlist enliven entertain enthuse empower evaluate excite explore express extend facilitate finance forgive foster franchise further gather generate give grant heal hold host identify illuminate implement improve improvise inspire integrate involve keep know labor launch lead light live love make manifest master mature measure mediate model mold motivate move negotiate nurture open organize participate pass perform persuade play possess practice praise prepare present produce progress promise promote provide pursue realize receive reclaim reduce refine reflect reform regard relate relax release rely remember renew resonate respect restore return revise sacrifice safeguard satisfy save sell serve share speak stand summon support surrender sustain take tap team touch trade translate travel understand use utilize validate value venture verbalize volunteer work worship write yield

— NOTES —

1   Rabbi Jonathan Sacks, *A Letter in the Scroll,* The Free Press, a division of Simon & Schuster 2000, 226.

2   Ibid., 92.

3   Plato, The Republic, in: The Dialogues of Plato, (Translated by J. Harwad), Great Books of the Western World, Encyclopedia Britannica, 1952. In Book 7 Socrates explains to Glaucon the allegory of living in a cave, where one could mistake the shadows on the wall of the cave as true reality rather than the original light source.

4   Lawrence Kushner, God was in this Place & I,I did not know, Jewish Lights Publishing,1991, 44.

5   Rabbi Albert Milton Kanter, Psychotheology, HTC Press, 1996, 77.

6   Plato, Apology, in: The Dialogues of Plato, (Translated by J. Harwad), Encyclopedia Britannica, 1952, 203.

7   Robert Kane, The Quest for Meaning, Values, Ethics and the Modern Experience, Tape Series ,The Teaching Company, Lecture 21.

8   Robert Kane, The Quest for Meaning, Values, Ethics and the Modern Experience, Tape Series ,The Teaching Company, Course Guide 44.

9   Stephen Covey, The 7 Habits of Highly Effective People, Fireside, Simon & Schuster,1989,71.

10   Mishnah Avot, Chapter 2, Mishnah 21.

11   Viktor Frankl, Man's Search for Meaning, Beacon Press, 1959,132.

12   Ibid., 84.

13   Adin Steinsaltz, Simple Words, Touchstone Book published by Simon and Schuster, 1999, 215.

14 *W. W. Rouse Ball, A Short Account of the History of Mathematics, (4th edition) 1908.*

15 Brian Tracy, Maximum Achievement, Simon & Schuster,1993, 29.

16 Dennis Prager, Happiness Is a Serious Problem, ReganBooks – Harper Collins, 3.

17 Ibid., 5.

18 Attributed to Einstein, see Alice Caliprice, The New Quotable Einstein, Princeton University Press, 2005 292. This quote may be a paraphrase of his 1946 quotation: "a new type of thinking is essential if mankind is to survive the move toward higher levels." (Nathan and Norden, Einstein on Peace, 383).

19 Robert Kiyosaki, Rich Dad Poor Dad, Warner Books, 1997, 125.

20 M. Scott Peck The Road Less Traveled, Touchtone Published by Simon & Schuster, 1978, 15.

21 Anthony Robbins, Lessons in Mastery, Nightingale Conant, Tape 2.

22 Brian Tracy, Success Is a Journey, Executive Excellence Publishing, 1999, 62.

23 Tal Ben-Shahar, Happier, McGraw-Hill, 2007, 33.

24 Ibid., 27.

25 Marci Shimoff, Happy for No Reason, Free Press, A Division of Simon & Schuster, 2008, 27.

26 Ibid., 4-5.

27 Ibid., 25-26.

28 Viktor Frankl, Man's Search for Meaning, 140.

29 Rob Stearns, Winning Smart After Losing Big, Encounter Books, 2003, 99.

30 Peter Senge, The Fifth Discipline, A Currency Book, Doubleday, 1990, 14.

31   Joel Osteen, Your Best Life Now, Faith Words, 2004,270.

32   Dennis Prager, Happiness Is a Serious Problem, 6.

33   Stephen Covey, The 7 Habits of Highly Effective People, 70.

34   Steven Goldman, Science Wars: What Scientists Know and How They Know It, Lecture Transcript and Course Guidebook, The Teaching Company, 2006, Part 1, 14.

35   Ibid.

36   Ibid., 15

37   Ibid., 17.

38   Jeffrey Kasser, Philosophy of Science, Lecture Transcript and Course Guidebook, The Teaching Company, 2006, Part 1, 12.

39   Steven Prothero. God is Not One, HarperCollins, 2010, 3.

40   Ibid., 11-12.

41   I have never been able to find where in the writings of Rumi this quote is found. It is often referenced as a statement by a Sufi teacher. Margaret Wheatly (Leadership and the New Science, Berrett-Koehler, 1992, 9) quotes Donellla Meadows (Whole Earth Models and Systems, Co-Evolution Quarterly, Summer 1982, 101).

42   Steven Goldman, Science Wars: What Scientists Know and How They Know It, Lecture Transcript and Course Guidebook, The Teaching Company, 2006, Part 1, 25-27.

43   The two other forms of this quotation are:

      1) There are "Two sorts of truth: trivialities, where opposites are obviously absurd and profound truths, recognized by the fact that the opposite is also a profound truth." As quoted by his son Hans Bohr in "My Father", published in Neils Bohr : His Life and Work (1967), p. 328.

2) It is the hallmark of any deep truth that its negation is also a deep truth. As quoted in Max Delbrück, *Mind from Matter: An Essay on Evolutionary Epistemology*, (1986) p. 167.

44 Ernest Kurtz and Katherine Ketcham, The Spirituality of Imperfection, Bantam Books, 1992, 60.

45 Gerald Schroeder, God According to God, HarperOne HarperCollins, 2009, 50-51.

46 Ibid., 225.

47 Ibid., 3.

48 Ibid., 18.

49 From Wikipedia, Monotheism http://en.wikipedia.org/wiki/Monotheism referenced 11-18-2010.

50 Paul Bender, Life's Holy Light, Manual of Holiday and Occasional Sermons, Rabbinical Council Press, 1944, 32-35.

51 Brian Greene, The Fabric of the Cosmos, Knopf, 2004, 225-226.

52 Gerald Schroeder, The Science of God, Broadway Books,1998, 161-165.

53 Hyrum Smith, The 10 Natural Laws of Successful Time and Life Management, Warner Books, 1994, 3.

54 Rabbi Jonathan Sacks, The Home We Build Together, Continuum, 2007, 115-116.

55 Ibid., 117.

56 Rabbi Jonathan Sacks, Covenant and Conversation - Pekudei 2010, http://www.chiefrabbi.org/ReadArtical.aspx?id=740.

57 Martin Buber, The Way of Man, Citadel Press, 1964, 36-37

58 Ernest Kurtz and Katherine Ketcham, The Spirituality of Imperfection, Bantam Books, 1992, 9-10 (and elsewhere).

59 Presentation on Perfectionism at the Pride institute, California, 1993.

60 Robert Kane, The Quest for Meaning, Values, Ethics and the Modern Experience, Tape Series ,The Teaching Company, Course Guide, Part 2, 61

61 Plato, The Symposium, in: The Dialogues of Plato, (translated by J. Harwad), Great Books of the Western World, Encyclopedia Britannica, 1952.

62 M. Scott Peck The Road Less Traveled, 81.

63 Mishnah Avot, Chapter 2, Mishnah 14.

64 Martin Buber, The Way of Man, 31

65 Ibid., 32.

66 Babylonian Talmud, 31a.

67 Robert Kane, The Quest for Meaning, Values, Ethics and the Modern Experience, Tape Series ,The Teaching Company, Course Guide Part 2, 10.

68 Tom Morris, If Aristotle Ran General Motors, Henry Holt, 1997,146-147.

69 Ernest Kurtz and Katherine Ketcham, The Spirituality of Imperfection, 231.

70 Gerhard Gschwandtner, Quoted in: Customer Care, Celebrating Excellence, 1992, 57.

71 Ernest Kurtz and Katherine Ketcham, The Spirituality of Imperfection, 95-96.

72 Stephen Covey, The 7 Habits of Highly Effective People, 235.

73 Ernest Kurtz and Katherine Ketcham, The Spirituality of Imperfection, 70.

74 Ibid., 87.

75 Lawrence Kushner, God was in this Place & I,I did not know, 71-76.

76 Viktor Frankl, Man's Search for Meaning, Beacon Press, 1959,132.

77 Ibid., 133.

78 Ibid., 135-136.

79 Samson Hirsch, The Pentateuch Volume3 Leviticus (part 1), Judaica Press, 1976, 394.

80 Ernest Kurtz and Katherine Ketcham, The Spirituality of Imperfection, 175.

81 Mordecai Kaplan, Basic Values in Jewish Religion, The Reconstructionist Press, 1948, 60.

82 Robert Emmons, Thanks, Houghton Mifflin, 2007, 4.

83 Ibid., 94-95.

84 Ibid., 110.

85 Ibid., 111.

86 Wayne Dyer, Manifest Your Destiny, HarperCollins, 1997, 150-152.

87 Ibid., 154-157.

88 Ernest Kurtz and Katherine Ketcham, The Spirituality of Imperfection, 184.

89 George Leonard, Mastery, Dutton Books-Penguin Books, 1991, 17.

90 Ibid., 48-49.

91 Ibid., 80.

92 Ibid., 76

93 Babylonian Talmud, Berachot, 64a.

94 Ernest Kurtz and Katherine Ketcham, The Spirituality of Imperfection, 81.

— INDEX —